PASSING FAITH'S TESTS WITH LOVE AND JOY

D0169480

A Study of James through Jude

Jack W. Hayford
with
Kathy A. Hagan

THOMAS NELSON PUBLISHERS
Nashville

Passing Faith's Tests with
Love and Joy
Copyright © 1997 by Jack W. Hayford

Published in Nashville, Tennessee, by Thomas Nelson, Inc.

Printed in the United States of America
2 3 4 5 6 7 8 — 02 01 00 99 98 97

CONTENTS

. . . .

Passing Faith's Tests with Love and Joy is one of a series of study guides that focus exciting, discovery-geared coverage of Bible book and power themes—all prompting toward dynamic, Holy Spirit-filled living.

About the Executive Editor

JACK W. HAYFORD, noted pastor, teacher, writer, and composer, is the Executive Editor of the complete series, working with the publisher in conceiving and developing each of the books.

Dr. Hayford is Senior Pastor of The Church On The Way, the First Foursquare Church of Van Nuys, California. He and his wife, Anna, have four married children, all of whom are active in either pastoral ministry or vital church life. As General Editor of the *Spirit-Filled Life® Bible*, Pastor Hayford led a four-year project which has resulted in the availability of one of today's most practical and popular study Bibles. He is author of more than twenty books, including *A Passion for Fullness, The Beauty of Spiritual Language, Rebuilding the Real You,* and *Prayer Is Invading the Impossible.* His musical compositions number over four hundred songs, including the widely sung "Majesty."

About the Writer

KATHY A. HAGAN is a Church of God minister and writer currently residing in Jackson, Mississippi. She holds both undergraduate and graduate degrees in education from Murray State University and was a teacher in the Henry County (Tennessee) School System for sixteen years. In 1994, Kathy received the Master of Divinity degree from the Church of God School of Theology in Cleveland, Tennessee, and has served her denomination as an Associate Pastor/Minister of Discipleship and itinerant Bible teacher. She is the writer of *Redemption and Restoration: Reversing Life's Greatest Losses,* the *Spirit-Filled Life® Bible Discovery Guide* on Ruth and Esther.

Kathy has a grown son and daughter-in-law, Jeff and Lori Hagan, who reside in Nashville, Tennessee.

THE GIFT
THAT KEEPS ON GIVING

One of the most precious gifts God has given us is His Word, the Bible. Wrapped in the glory and sacrifice of His Son and delivered by the power and ministry of His Spirit, it is a treasured gift—the gift that keeps on giving, because the Giver it reveals is inexhaustible in His love and grace.

Tragically, though, fewer and fewer people are opening this gift and seeking to understand what it's all about and how to use it. They often feel intimidated by it. It requires some assembly, and its instructions are hard to comprehend sometimes. How does the Bible fit together anyway? What does this ancient Book have to say to us who are looking toward the twenty-first century?

Will taking the time and energy to understand its instructions and to fit it all together really help you and me?

Yes. Yes. Without a shred of doubt.

The *Spirit-Filled Life® Bible Discovery Guide* series is designed to help you unwrap, assemble, and enjoy all God has for you in the pages of Scripture. It will focus your time and energy on the books of the Bible, the people and places they describe, and the themes and life applications that flow thick from its pages like honey oozing from a beehive.

So you can get the most out of God's Word, this series has a number of helpful features:

 WORD WEALTH

"WORD WEALTH" provides definitions of key terms.

BEHIND THE SCENES

"BEHIND THE SCENES" supplies information about cultural practices, doctrinal disputes, business trades, etc.

AT A GLANCE

"AT A GLANCE" features helpful maps and charts.

BIBLE EXTRA

"BIBLE EXTRA" will guide you to other resources that will enable you to glean more from the Bible's wealth.

PROBING THE DEPTHS

"PROBING THE DEPTHS" will explain controversial issues raised by particular lessons and cite Bible passages and other sources to help you come to your own conclusions.

FAITH ALIVE

The "FAITH ALIVE" feature will help you see and apply the Bible to your day-to-day needs.

The only resources you need to complete and apply these study guides are a heart and mind open to the Holy Spirit, a prayerful attitude, and a pencil and a Bible. Of course, you may draw upon other sources, but these study guides are comprehensive enough to give you all you need to gain a good, basic understanding of the Bible book being covered and how you can apply its themes and counsel to your life.

A word of warning, though. By itself, Bible study will not transform your life. It will not give you power, peace, joy, comfort, hope, and a number of other gifts God longs for you to unwrap and enjoy. Through Bible study, you will grow in your understanding of the Lord, His kingdom and your place in it, but you must be sure to rely on the Holy Spirit to guide your study and your application of the Bible's truths. He, Jesus promised, was sent to teach us "all things" (John 14:26; cf. 1 Cor. 2:13). Bathe your study time in prayer, asking the Spirit of God to illuminate the text, enlighten your mind, humble your will, and comfort your heart. He will never let you down.

My prayer and goal for you is that as you unwrap and begin to explore God's Book for living His way, the Holy Spirit will fill every fiber of your being with the joy and power God longs to give all His children. So read on. Be diligent. Stay open and submissive to Him. You will not be disappointed. He promises you!

Lesson 1/ Test: Joyfully Growing in the Midst of Trials and Temptations
(James 1:1–27)

Not long after becoming a Christian in young adulthood, I "found" Psalm 139 and claimed it as my own special treasure. In the aura of new, immature love for God, I was thrilled by the fact of His all-knowingness, His ever-present care and protection, His continual sustenance. I rejoiced in the knowledge that even before my birth, God had designed a special plan and purpose for my life. Greedily, I drank in the words of Psalm 139 and the comforting, healing love they described. Yet I didn't understand the last part of the psalm. There, in essence, David cries: "If only You would get rid of all my enemies and every adversity!" Then, touched by insight, David humbly requests: "Uncover all my anxieties and hidden sin that I may truly walk in the way of everlasting life."

Immature Christians want the "easy side" of God's love which asks little of them and doesn't test their faith. But James shows that it is the adversities of life which prove our faith. And it is our response to the enticements of the enemies of the soul which reveal the true foundation and integrity of our love for God.

In chapter 1, James teaches that we can joyfully grow in the midst of trials and temptations if we understand the purpose, provisions, and potential of trials (1:1–12); refuse to fall prey to temptations (1:13–18); and listen and do the word of God (1:19–27).

OVERVIEW OF THE EPISTLE OF JAMES

Before beginning the first lesson in James, complete a quick reading of the entire epistle. Then, study the information provided in the chart. Add information after each question mark.

THE EPISTLE OF JAMES[1]
From: James, the brother of Jesus and leader of the church at Jerusalem *a servant of God*
To? *the 12 tribes in the Dispersion (Jews)*
Date Written: Sometime between A.D. 48, just before the Jerusalem Council (Acts 15), and A.D. 62, when James was martyred.
Special Feature: The book of James is an instruction book with similarities to the Proverbs and the Sermon on the Mount (Matt. 5—7). It contains 54 clear commands.
Repeated Words and Phrases? *doer, faith, trial, endure*
Key Verse? " *Faith without works is dead* ." (James 2:17)
Overall Message? *humble service to God's people is evidence of a faith relationship*

James could have identified himself as Jesus' brother or an eyewitness of the resurrected Lord or leader of the Jerusalem church. How does he describe himself? What does this designation tell you about James? How does it fit the overall message of the book? (1:1) *servants to the will of their master. James wants to be a humble servant — not gaining prestige from his position as Jesus' brother.*

UNDERSTAND THE PURPOSE, PROVISION, AND POTENTIAL OF TRIALS (JAMES 1:2–12)

The modern Western world has often painted a picture of Christianity which suggests that coming to Christ will separate one from the trials and tribulations commonly encountered in life in this fallen world. James, like his colleagues in the gospel, announces that Christians will indeed suffer trials. Yet he shows that every trial is alive with opportunity to grow strong and tall in faith. For a Christian, adversity bears a purpose, includes a provision, and possesses a glorious potential!

What is the attitude a Christian should express when encountering any variety of trials? (1:2; also see 1 Pet. 4:12, 13)

Count it all joy! Rejoice!

What is the basis, or cause, of this attitude? (1:3)

testing of faith produces steadfastness

WORD WEALTH

Count it all joy (James 1:2): "Count" (*hēgeomai*, Strong's *#2233*) could be translated "consider, deem, reckon, evaluate, or judge." Therefore, the phrase does not describe a forced or flippant emotional reaction (see 1 Pet. 1:3–6), but a seasoned judgment of the will and mind based on an understanding of the purpose of trials. Out of this base of knowledge comes true rejoicing in anticipation of the glorious results the trial will produce.

What do trials test? Produce? (1:3)

faith   steadfastness (patience)

WORD WEALTH

Patience (1:3), *hupomonē* (Strong's *#5281*), comes from a verb meaning "to hold one's ground in conflict, bear up against adversity, hold out under stress, persevere under pressure."[2] It may best be translated "perseverance" or "endurance." This type of patience is "not a passive resignation to adverse circumstances, but a positive steadfastness that bravely endures."[3] It is an active, strong, and unshakable trust in God that finds its base in belief in the integrity of God's character, His word, and His care.

Picture an athlete such as an Olympic runner, swimmer, or weight lifter. Think about the mental and physical process he goes through to develop the stamina necessary to perform well. How could you relate this picture to spiritual endurance produced by encountering trials?

List the three ways in which patience's "perfect work" is defined. (1:4)

1. *perfect*

2. *complete*

3. *lacking in nothing*

Given the three adjectives above, it is obvious that James is not talking about "perfection" in terms of complete sinlessness. Together the words indicate a steadfast relationship to God, a fully developed cluster of fruit of the Spirit, and a life which consistently shows no lack of holiness or works of obedience.[4] What word(s) would you use to describe a Christian fitting this description? (1:4; see "perfect" in Gen. 6:9; 17:1; Job 1:1; 2:3) *righteous, blameless; upright, God-fearing one who turns away from evil*

BIBLE EXTRA

Read the following verses and jot down the way in which the full work of patience, or perseverance, is further defined elsewhere.

Romans 5:3–5 *suffering - endurance - Character - hope*

2 Corinthians 4:16,17 *temporal affliction prepares us for eternal glory beyond compare*

Hebrews 10:36 *need endurance to do God's will so to receive what's been promised*

1 Peter 1:7 *faith tested by fire to last till the End.*

In verse 2, James tells us to **do something** (<u>rejoice</u> when trials come) because we **know something** (trials can produce perseverance). In verse 4, he tells us to **allow something** (let patience do its complete work in our lives). This "letting" sounds like a deliberate act of the will. How could your will be involved in getting the greatest growth out of a trial? Preventing your growth? *Being anxious can diminish my faith - reduces trust. But patience, puts all trust in God that He will work in my life*

What provision does God make to help one successfully persevere in a trial? (1:5) *We can ask God for wisdom!*

WORD WEALTH

Wisdom (James 1:5), *sophia* (Strong's *#4678*), is a <u>practical wisdom</u> which works with knowledge but goes beyond it. It is a <u>comprehensive insight</u> into the true nature of a particular situation which leads to a correct and skillful application of knowledge.[5] In short, this wisdom reveals what to do. On one hand, it helps one to avoid a wrong, sinful response. On the other hand, it directs one toward the way of righteousness.

Without this kind of wisdom, one may waste the opportunity God has given for growth in spiritual maturity. For this reason, one should keep asking for and applying wisdom throughout the trial. (See: Rom. 8:25–27, which shows that the Holy Spirit joins in the agonizing prayer offered during adversity and makes it effective.)

Describe the limits which define God's willingness to give this wisdom. To whom will He give it? When? How much? (1:5)

all men, generously, w/o reproach

What is the only restriction placed on receiving wisdom from God? (1:6, 7) *ask in faith, do not doubt*

What fundamental belief is the basis of confidence in prayer? (1:2, 3, 5; also Rom. 8:31–38) *God loves us, hears us, and cannot be separated from us*

Study the images and characteristics of "the doubter" (1:6–8). In your own words, describe what each one means.

"a wave of the sea driven and tossed by the wind" (1:6) *shaky faith*

"double-minded (or dual-souled) man" (1:8) *evil still controls*

"unstable in all his ways" (1:8) *not steadfast*

What would the doubter likely do with wisdom—specific insight and direction—if God gave it to him/her?
Use it for evil? Squander it?

What two "trying" sets of circumstances are described in James 1:9–11? How would each test faith?
lowly   exalted
rich · humbled

What is the "exaltation" of the poor and the "humiliation" of the rich which James commands? The end-purpose, or potential, in James's instruction for both socioeconomic categories of Christians? (1:9–11)
Get the poor doing well enough that they can consider more than their physical survival. Get the rich to see that they "can't take it with them". Get them both to trust God

What is the resultant state of the Christian who remains steadfast in faith and the love of God in trials? (Note: The word translated "temptation" here in KJV and NKJV is the same Greek word translated "trials" in James 1:2.) (1:12)

eternal glory in heaven, with God "crown of life"

WORD WEALTH

Blessed (James 1:12): *makarios* (Strong's #3107), sometimes translated "happy" or "prosperous," has a meaning which transcends either of these English words. It is an enduring condition or state of joy and satisfaction which is worthy of congratulations, and describes the "distinctive joy which comes through participation in the divine kingdom." [6]

List the three things this blessed person has done.

1. *endures trials*

2. *stood the test*

3. *loves God*

How is "loving God" foundational to the other two actions listed above? *Reason to even try to endure - in response to Jesus sacrifice for us*

What is the promised reward for persevering steadfast in faith? *"crown of life" - eternal life with Jesus (also improved relationship with God while here)*

BIBLE EXTRA

The crown of life (James 1:12): During the New Testament era, "crown" *(stephanos)* was most often associated with athletic competition and the wreath of greenery which was placed on the head of the victor. But in Christianity, "crown" was used in a metaphorical sense as the "eternal reward" the faithful would receive (1 Cor. 9:25; 2 Tim. 2:5; 4:8). The "crown of life" mentioned in Revelations 2:10 is used in this sense. It is "the crown which is life" promised to the persecuted who are "faithful unto death" and can be equated with the resurrection life seen in the One "who died and came to life" (Rev. 2:8).

In James, the "crown of life" is more than the eternal life one receives at salvation (John 5:24) or the immortal life to be received at Christ's return. The phrase "when he has been approved" or "after he has been tested and proved" marks time and shows that something in this life is to be received. Since it is a Christian accomplishment following initial salvation and prior to the return, it must reflect a superior quality of Christian life which may be related to the spiritual maturity promised to those who persevere (1:4) and the blessed state of the overcomer (see James 5:10, 11). It, too, is a "crown which is life"—a deeper participation in the life of God and the joys of the kingdom of God.

The victor here—who has continued to love God and follow the wisdom of God (1:5, 12)—must be seen in contrast to "the one who is led away by his own evil lusts" described in the passage which follows (1:13–15). Perhaps this victorious one is most clearly described in Romans 8:28 (which see). Every situation, circumstance, and trial, no matter how large or small, works out for the optimum good, bringing him/her forward in Christian life and maturity.[7]

DON'T FALL PREY TO TEMPTATION (JAMES 1:13–18)

James 1:1–12 shows that trials which test one's faith will come to Christians in the form of adverse outward circumstances, situations, and events. These are opportune times to gain strength and grow in Christian wisdom and maturity. But at these times, one is also especially vulnerable. Adversity reveals what one is truly made of! It tests faith to its core! Anger, bad attitudes, and evil desires of which one was not previously aware, often surface. If faith in God is weak and shaken, if one does not turn to God for strength and heed His wisdom, that one may fall prey to temptations.

What emphatic statement is James making in this entire section of text? (1:13–18, especially 13)

God does NOT tempt us — it is our own sinful nature

How would you define temptation? What is the difference between trials and temptations in terms of source and end-product? (1:2–4, 13–15)

Temptation: the desire to fulfil evil internal ideas.

temptation - internal/self   trials - outward/world

Why is it impossible for God to solicit anyone to sin? (1:17)

God is good — the Giver of good

Scripture shows that enticement to sin may come from the world, the flesh, or the devil, but where does James soundly lay the responsibility for sin? (1:14)

from within one's self

AT A GLANCE

Read James 1:14 and 15 and 2 Corinthians 10:5. Then study the chart below.

THE PROGRESS OF SIN (James 1:14, 15)				
Emotions	**Mind**	**Will**	**Body**	**Whole Person**
Feelings —>	Conception of Sin: —>	Birth —>	Pattern —>	Death: Seared
of Desire	Entertains idea.	of	of	Conscience,
or Need	Makes plans to	Outward	Ongoing	Reprobate
Enticement to	carry out the sin.	Act	Sin	Mind, Diseased
Satisfy Need	Rationalizes the	of	Creates	Body, Spiritual
or Alter	sinfulness of sin.	Sin	Stronghold	Death
Feelings by				
Illegitimate				
Means				

Where and how does temptation conceive? What is the most effective point at which to stop the progress toward sin? Why? *When you recognize that the emotion is producing a sinful effect - when it first enters the mind - so that you may not sin in thought.*

Under the following headings, describe the motivations James offers for refusing temptation and surrendering to God.

Consequences of Temptation (1:15): *Death*

God's Character and Gifts (1:17): *Good, Good*

Believer's Current Testimony Concerning God (1:18a): *God brought us to believe through His Word*

Consequences of Life with God (1:18b): *We would be a kind of first fruits of his creatures."*

 FAITH ALIVE

Adversity comes to everyone. People lose career jobs, natural disasters occur, family members move far away, relationships break down, loved ones die, the hoped-for break never comes. What does it mean to you, in such times, to know that God does not change? Write your thoughts as a praise to Him. *You love me Lord - You will take care of me - I am never far from Your thoughts*

LISTEN AND DO THE WORD OF GOD (JAMES 1:19–27) *Amen!*

Here James further contrasts the two ways of responding to adversity: gaining wisdom from God or reacting angrily to the pressures, feelings, and fears produced by difficult times. He shows that the path to true faith and spiritual growth is to listen and do the Word of God.

Read James 1:19–27 and Romans 10:17. Why is faithful "hearing"—or listening and doing—so important in the Christian life? *It is evidence of faith in Him.*

James shows that one must make preparations for true hearing of the Word. What must be released, restrained, and removed? (1:19–21a)

wickedness   *pride*   *anger*

wildness

Why is anger useless and destructive in the kingdom of God? (1:20, 21; 3:18; Col. 3:8)

- does not work for righteousness of God
- in peace (not anger) is the harvest of righteousness sown

FAITH ALIVE

Before anger becomes full-blown and spews over into moral filth and wickedness, there are warning signs which indicate that one is drifting from God. Use this checklist to help examine your heart during trials:

_____ Am I beginning to lose the desire to pray?

_____ Have my personal devotions become sporadic or "dry"?

_____ Have I begun looking for excuses to miss gathering with the body of Christ to hear the Word of God?

_____ Do I find myself doing a lot of complaining?

_____ Am I generally "unhappy" or "irritable"? Does my temper have a shorter fuse than normal?

_____ Have the things of the world (possessions, money, power, status) become more important to me?

_____ Have I begun to be drawn to the "old way of thinking" or the "old way of life" I followed before I knew Jesus as Savior or before I reached this point of Christian maturity?

In order for the Word to be received, what quality must be added to a clean life, a quiet heart, and a receptive mind? (1:21) *meekness*

What is the power and purpose of receiving the Word? (1:21) *to save my soul from hell*

BIBLE EXTRA

The Parable of the Soils and Receiving the Word (James 1:19–27, Mark 4:1–20): Study the four soils of the parable Jesus said was foundational to understanding all parables. What may keep one from receiving the Word of God? From growing the Word? *Satan, cares of the world / desires, not feeding the faith*

How does the description of the "good soil" and its harvest help explain James's statement that one who listens without doing the Word is deceived about his/her spiritual life? (Mark 4:20; James 1:22) *The one who receives the Word, bears good fruit for all to see.*

James shows that the Word is a two-way mirror. We look into it, and it looks into us. What does seeing the "natural face" mean in spiritual terms? (1:23) *Seeing our soul — including the depth of our relationship with God.*

How is this "seeing" function related to "the perfect law of liberty"? From what does it "give freedom"? (1:23–25; Ps. 119:11) *If we "see" the honor in our souls — we will turn to God and be free from sin.*

What is the difference between one who never looks into the "mirror" and one who looks but does not comb disheveled hair or remove the smudge on the cheek? Is the second person's religious activity genuine? Why? (1:22–24, 26, 27)

→ The first has no clue as to what he is like.

The second knows the law, but ignores it and therefore ignores God.

James shows that the Word reveals our sin and character flaws and sets us free from them. What other mirror function of the Word is revealed in 2 Corinthians 3:16–18? Why is this additional function so important as it relates to "doing true religion"? (1:27; 2 Cor. 3:16–18)

We see God with the veil removed. We know what we should strive for because we see the perfect example – our Lord, Himself

What two actions are companions of an empty religion? What two actions are companions of a true, ethical, and unblemished religion? (1:26, 27)

doing good to others and keeping oneself pure!

wagging tongue deceived heart

FAITH ALIVE

Generally, what is your first action when a trial hits? Do you react emotionally or do you respond deliberately?

Pray

then I try to

Place an "x" on the line to show your position as a trial continues:

I lose faith in God's	I continually vacillate	I remain
←---goodness and-----------	-----between----------	-X-steadfast ---→
willingness to help.	faith and doubt.	in faith.

Based on the truth gleaned from James 1, outline your plan of action to start and continue faithfully in adversities. Apply that plan to a recent trial that stressed your faith or one you are experiencing now.

I will continue to pray and praise. I will continue to search for the job and keep my house well – I will continue to believe

Two kinds of "heroes of faith" are mentioned in Hebrews 11. One experiences miraculous deliverance; one endures adver-

that God will take care of us!

sity while seeing no visible relief. How would you "hold up" *I don't know* under the afflictions of the second group? Are you willing to have this kind of character and unshakable faith developed in your life? *yes* Speak to God concerning your fears and your desire for faith that passes every test.

What have you learned about God in your study of James 1? How will this new knowledge of Him affect your life today? For the future?

God wants me to want to know more of Him. He also wants my faith to endure in trials and to produce good works.

God loves me and will not fail in His promise of eternal life through Jesus.

He is always with me in trials. He wants me to be pure.

I will trust, pray and draw near to God - today and always. And if I should fail, I pray that God could call me back into a close relationship w/ Him.

1. *Spirit-Filled Life Bible* (Nashville: Thomas Nelson Publishers, 1991), 1893, "Author" and "Date."

2. Ibid., 1451, "Word Wealth: Matt. 24:13, endures."

3. Ibid., 1895, Notes on James 1:3.

4. Fritz Rienecker and Cleon Rogers, *Linguistic Key to the Greek New Testament* (Grand Rapids: Zondervan Publishing House, 1980), 721.

5. *Spirit-Filled Life Bible*, 1636, "Word Wealth: Acts 6:10, wisdom."

6. Gerhard Kittel and Gerhard Friedrich, eds. *Theological Dictionary of the New Testament* (Grand Rapids: William B. Eerdmans Publishing Company, 1985), Abridged in One Volume by Geoffrey W. Bromiley, 548–549. Also, *Spirit-Filled Life Bible*, 1410, "Word Wealth: Matt. 5:3, blessed."

7. Donald W. Burdick, *James, The Expositor's Bible Commentary*, Vol. 12 (Grand Rapids: Zondervan Publishing House, 1981), 170–171. C. J. Homer, "Crown, Sceptre, Rod," *The New International Dictionary of New Testament Theology*, ed. Colin Brown (Grand Rapids: Zondervan Publishing House, 1986), 1:405–406.

Lesson 2/Test: Showing Evidence of True Faith (James 2:1—3:18)

It is easy to become captivated by the suspense of a live courtroom drama. The intensity builds to the finale of the case: the reading of the verdict. The judge asks for the jury's written decision. The courtroom grows still. The tension is palpable as the judge commands the defendant to rise.

At that moment, the works of a lifetime hang in the balance. The defendant's accomplishments may be shattered into a heap of rubbish by the verdict arrived at by hearing spoken testimony and eyewitness accounts and viewing material evidence. The thoughts, emotions, and intentions of the defendant have no validity in face of the weight of evidence. Only verifiable evidence which proves the truth of the defendant's claims counts.

In a similar vein, James declares that true faith generates evidence. He shows that a superficial faith or an empty religion will betray itself by the works it fails to produce. Good intentions, high-minded words, and stirred religious emotions have little validity if they do not result in a life of active faith. In chapters two and three, James states that real faith will show the verifiable evidences of: a love that keeps the royal law (2:1–13), a faith that works (2:14–26), a maturity which results in controlled speech (3:1–12), and a true wisdom which is lived out in humility (3:13–18).

THE TEST OF LOVE: KEEPING THE "ROYAL LAW" (JAMES 2:1–13)

It would be highly unlikely in this day and age that any local church could exist which has not been affected to some degree by the situation James presents in the first few verses of chapter 2. Here, James makes a strong case for the necessity of demonstrating impartial Christian love. He argues first from the standpoint of the Christian's relationship to Jesus Christ. Then he proceeds with social and moral arguments and ends with a resounding warning to all who may be tempted to forsake the "royal law."

What is the situation James is denouncing and his main message as it relates to this situation? (2:1–13; especially 1–4)

Giving higher regard to those with $, prestige and power, than to those with less or none.

WORD WEALTH

"Partiality" (James 2:1, 9) comes from the verb *prosōpolēpteō* (Strong's #4380) which literally reads "to receive the face" or "to lay hold of a face."[1] In modern language, we might relate it to "taking something at face value" or using a superficial means of evaluating people based on outward appearances. Such partiality, or favoritism, may be founded on physical beauty, apparel, gender, race, occupation, social position, material wealth, or other forms of power and influence.

What two things does James show to be incompatible? (2:1)   *Faith in Jesus and showing particality on worldly charateristics*

Why might favoritism be more likely in a very small or "economically challenged" church like the one James addresses here? (2:1–4) *That church may "need" the $ more to survive.*

Is the treatment given the rich visitor wrong? Why or why not? (2:2, 3, 6) *No – we should love all of our neighbors*

How does James describe the root of the difference made between rich and poor? (2:4) *The problem comes when we dishonor the poor by treating them differently than the rich.*

What might be the evil reasoning, or internal dialogue, of those showing favoritism? What does that say about the foundation of their faith? *Evil reasoning - Be nice, get bucks. Don't we trust God to provide, by the moving of hearts, for our ministry ????*

What false images of the poor and the rich do those showing favoritism possess? (2:5–7; 1:9) *That the rich are more blessed by God — when in reality God blesses the poor with greater faith.*

What three actions characteristic of the rich and unlikely of the poor prove this favoritism to be irrational? (2:6, 7) *Rich - oppress others, more likely to sue, more likely to forget that God is the Source of their riches, not their hard work.*

James shows partiality to be a deeper error than wrong social perception. Favoritism in the body of Christ is morally wrong and a violation of the "royal law." Contrast the royal law and partiality by their actions, character, and end results. (2:8–11)

THE ROYAL LAW VS. PARTIALITY (2:8–11)		
	Action **Character**	**End Result**
Royal Law:	*Love your neighbor* *full of your mercy?/ours* *as self*	*Mercy*
Partiality:	*Love some neighbors better than others ...* *Sinful merciless*	*Judgment*

BIBLE EXTRA

The Royal Law (James 2:8) is the "king of laws" which ancient Hebrew teachers, Jesus, and Paul all affirmed as the "great command" which brings together and puts into action all the instruction of the law and the prophets. To keep this royal law of "loving your neighbor as yourself" is to fully express God's will for human relationships. Such obedience finds its <u>foundation in love for God and is the outflow of the love of God</u>. Thus, when James states that disobedience to an individual relational command is breaking the whole law, he is not saying that one is guilty of committing each individual relational sin. Rather, to act in any way against or outside of this royal law of love is rebellion against God and His comprehensive will and intention for humankind (James 2:9–11). (See: ancient teachings: Lev. 19:15–18; Ex. 20:12–17; Jesus' teaching: Mark 12:28–31; also Matt. 5:43 and 7:12, Luke 10:25–28; Paul's teaching: Rom. 13:8–10; Gal. 5:14.)[2]

In James 1:25, the "perfect law of liberty" set the believer free from sin. How does it free one here? (2:12)

If you act and speak as one forgiven ...

Read Matthew 25:33–40 and reread James 2:12 and 13. How will compassion be victorious over judgment?

Compassion that leads to works will show one mercy, and God will show mercy to those who have shown it to others!

FAITH ALIVE

James uses the illustration of "a well-dressed man wearing a gold ring." What scenario would describe the way partiality is shown in your local church? Who are the "elite" and the "poor" in your congregation? *The church (or whole) welcomes the poor, as a whole. If you act differently they may talk about it.*

What underlying false beliefs concerning grace, salvation, inheritance, and judgment are revealed by this partiality?

That old traditional ways are the only way to act that is pleasing to God.

According to what you have learned here, what is the basis of acceptance and only judge of status in the body of Christ? *The condition of your head regarding your relationship with Jesus*

How can you begin to live in light of James's prohibition (2:1) and command (2:12)? What will you do differently this week? Commit your plans to God in prayer. *Accept different forms of worship and defend these who worship with their whole heart even when it means thistle in church.*

THE TEST OF SAVING FAITH: FAITH THAT WORKS (JAMES 2:14–26)

In this section of text, James presents the main message of his epistle. He picks up and expands the discussion of faith which he began in chapter 1, verses 21 through 27. Here, he poses the very questions which are today being asked by evangelists and leaders desiring to see powerful national and world-wide revival: What kind of faith is able to save? Is it enough to believe the right things about Jesus? Is it enough to be deeply touched and make a profession of faith? Or, is more required of saving faith?

Considering the only "evidence" of the faith described in verses 14 through 17, would you say this inadequate faith was a matter of the emotions, affections, mind, mouth, or will? Why so? (2:14–17) *Emotions & Mouth - I bet they were truly concerned for the ill clad malnourished bro & sis, but like so many lacked the courage or "true faith" to get involved.*

Given the example of verses 15 and 16, how would you support James's claim that this kind of faith is "unable to save," "unprofitable," and "dead"? (2:14-17) *A lack of true trust in Gods promises to be a truly living faith - yes - I agree with James*

James moves from a description of an empty profession to describe a faith of doctrinal confession and fear. Read the following references. Then, list the proper beliefs this "demonic" faith confesses. (James 2:19, 20; Mark 3:11, 12; Mark 5:1–13; Luke 8:31) *Jesus is God Almighty - to be worshiped and feared!*

Is such "faith" a matter of the intellect, emotions, affections, actions, or will? How does a faith of confession of creeds prove to be less than saving faith? (2:19, 20) *Intellect - the knowing of who God is and His power.*

Study the examples of saving faith seen in the accounts of Abraham and Rahab (James 2:21–25; Gen. 15:1–6, 22:1–12; Josh. 2, 6:22–25). How did each verify their faith in God? To what depths did Abraham and Rahab's faith reach: the emotions, mind, affections, will, actions? *All depths - emotion and mind faith led to will and action.*

Abraham was prepared/willing to sacrifice his son. Rahab to save the spies. Rescue her life.

Why must saving faith be profession + belief + works? (2:18, 22, 26; see also Matt. 7:21 and Eph. 2:8–10) *One completes/enhances the others - proves the others' existence.*

WORD WEALTH

"**Working together**" (James 2:22; *sunergeō,* Strong's #4903) shows the cooperation of faith and works in that each corroborates and assists the other in a "practical harmony" and a "powerful synergism." Saving faith creates works. In turn, works complete (fill full or perfect) faith.3

FAITH ALIVE

Which type of faith describes your life with God: good intentions (2:14–17), right confession (2:18–20), or the active life of faith (2:21–26)? How would you like that to change? *All three. - I want my faith to become more active in love all the time!*

What Christian conviction have you felt strongly or spoken passionately about but never put into action (e.g., evangelism, racial reconciliation, helping the poor)? What step(s) will you take this week to move from empty faith to a provable faith that works? *I act, but not enough/deeply enough. - Keep looking for an active-faith church where there are opportunities to reach out to the world - Keep trying to meet neighbors...*

THE TEST OF MATURITY: FAULTLESS SPEECH (JAMES 3:1–12)

In chapter 1, James cautioned readers to be "slow to speak." He showed that "an uncontrolled tongue and a deceived heart are companions of an empty religion" (1:19, 26, 27).[4] Now, in chapter 3, James exhorts readers, especially teachers, to give evidence of true faith and spiritual maturity by controlling their tongues. He describes the tongue's great power to influence and direct (3:1–4), its great power to destroy (3:5–8), and its great potential for good (3:9–12).

In terms of both the present and the eternal, why is it dangerous to lightly assume the role of teacher? Why do you think James singled out this particular role when talking to the church about the tongue? (3:1; see Matt. 23)

What is the one distinguishing mark of a "perfect" (sound or mature) Christian? And what two larger victories does this mark reveal? (3:2)

Contrast the nature, actions, and usefulness of a wild horse and a tamed, bridled horse. Then, relate these observations to speech and the Christian life. (3:3)

A ship guided by a rudder overcomes adverse winds, waves, and ocean currents. What does this picture imply concerning the power and influence of a mature Christian life? What does the converse imply about the danger of an uncontrolled tongue? (3:4)

List the evil characteristics and destructive works of the natural, untamed tongue mentioned in James 3:5–8. Then read James 3:9–11, and add the additional characteristic and evil work described there.

Characteristics of a Natural, Untamed Tongue

1.   6.

2.   7.

3.   8.

4.   9.

5.   10.

Destructive Works of the Untamed Tongue

1.   3.

2.   4.

What is the source behind the "unruly evil" and "deadly poison" of the tongue? (3:6)

Looking at the positive benefits of a fresh-water stream in an arid land and a fig tree or grapevine, what potential for good is possible when the tongue is blameless and controlled? (3:9–12; see also Prov. 10:11a, 21a, and 12:18b)

BIBLE EXTRA

Faultless Speech: In chapters 1 and 3 of the Book of James, we see that James affirms our Lord's statement that "out of the abundance of the heart the mouth speaks" (Matt. 12:34). James shows by antithesis that faultless speech springs from a pure heart which is not deceived (1:26). Such speech consistently praises God by vocally worshiping Him and speaking to and about others with respectful, refreshing, and edifying words which affirm the fact that humans are made in the image of God (3:9–12).

Understanding that deceit and evil may lurk in the heart, the truly religious and mature saint stands each day before the mirror of Scripture, letting the Word and the Holy Spirit examine hidden attitudes, motives, and actions (1:23–25; Jer. 17:9). Throughout the day, he/she is "slow to speak" and monitors every word before it is uttered (1:19; 3:2–4).[5]

FAITH ALIVE

When and in what ways have you experienced the devastation of a "great fire" set off by someone's words? Your own words? How have you experienced the healing, edifying power of the tongue in your Christian life?

What is the Holy Spirit saying to you personally concerning the use of your own tongue? Your maturity? What will you do about it? How will you be accountable?

TEST OF TRUE WISDOM: ACTIVE HUMILITY (JAMES 3:13–18)

As James continues his exhortations, he turns to the subject of true wisdom, contrasting it with a lower wisdom which in reality is not wisdom at all. Although his instruction is meant for all his readers, his topic is decidedly pointed toward teachers or leaders. One would expect this group, above all the people, to be "wise and understanding."

Read James's command in verse 13 and rewrite it in your own words. Then compare your statement with the message of 2:17.

WORD WEALTH

"**The meekness of wisdom**" (James 3:13) describes the manner in which a truly wise person's works are done. *Praütēs* (Strong's *#4240*), translated "meekness, humility, or gentleness," may describe the state of an animal which has been tamed so that its power is brought under control and directed in a useful manner. Here in 3:13, it is used in contrast to actions motivated by selfishness and pride. In James 1:21, it describes a readiness to receive instruction from the Word. Just as *sophia* (see "Word Wealth: "wisdom," Lesson 1) is the proper and insightful application of knowledge, *praütēs* is the proper and insightful application of power. Such "meekness" is an evidence of salvation and the continuing work of the Spirit. Such "wisdom" is the liberal gift of God to a growing Christian (1:5). Together these terms describe a possibility and manner of life and conduct which is conformed to Christ and empowered by the Holy Spirit.[6]

What is the "truth" about the counterfeit wisdom described in verse 14? Of what, therefore, would this person boast? (3:14, 15)

Fill in the blank by naming the type of worldly wisdom described.

Worldly Wisdom (James 3:15)

Origin:_____	natural, unregenerated
Life Focus:_____	having to do with the five senses and this present life
Underlying Character:_____	in agreement with Satan and his rebellious ways

Now compare James 3:15 to Ephesians 2:1–3. What conclusion can you draw concerning growth and spiritual life?

What are the products of envy and selfish ambition?

THE PROGRESSION OF DEMONIC "WISDOM" (3:13–15)	
HEART: ↓	**Bitter envy and self-seeking** (zeal or passion for ministry and the Lord is polluted or made "bitter" by hidden jealousy and rivalry; see 3:11), leading to
MOUTH: ↓	**Boasting** (sinful comparisons characterized by criticism of others and self-exaltation), leading to
LIFE and WITNESS: ↓	**Deceit/hypocrisy** (blindness to the truth concerning one's own spiritual condition), leading to
CHURCH COMMUNITY:	**Confusion and every evil thing** (disorder, instability, and every kind of sin and disruption).

Given the above progression and the magnitude of effect this "wisdom" may have on the local assembly and its mission, what weight would you now give to the James 3:13 command and Proverbs 4:7?

What is the origin and focus of true wisdom? What is at the base of its character and expression? (3:17)

WORD WEALTH

Pure (James 3:17)—"morally clean, faultless"—(*hagnos,* Strong's *#53*) shares the same root as "holy" (*hagios,* Strong's *#40*) which bears the idea of being fully separated unto God and His purposes. It is clear in James that wisdom which is *hagnos* must go beyond consecration of heart and sincerity of purpose. It must manifest itself in visible acts of holiness which bring health, peace, and selfless service to the faith community.

How do wisdom's end products compare to the products of worldly wisdom? Galatians' fruit of the Spirit? (3:16, 17; Gal. 5:22, 23)

What phrase in 3:18 is synonymous with "done in the meekness of wisdom"? (3:13, 18)

What problem does it seem James was confronting in the churches? What seems to be the solution to this problem? (3:18; also 3:1–17)

 ### FAITH ALIVE

James shows that zeal for the Lord/ministry may be carnal and worldly or spiritual and full of wisdom. How would you evaluate your zeal? Are you a help or a hindrance to the unity and mission of your local church? How so?

Test yourself. When you serve on a committee or hold a position, do you:

• rebel inwardly (if not outwardly) against the direction the group takes if it differs from your suggestion *or* graciously submit and work diligently toward a plan that was not your personal preference?

- rejoice when others succeed, hurt when they fail *or* envy and criticize others while secretly hoping they will fall short of your ability?

- have an attitude of gratefulness and feel a humility when chosen to serve *or* expect to be selected and feel wronged if someone else is appointed in "your place"?

- feel a need to be recognized for what you do *or* make it a point to affirm others' work and try to promote them?

- make sure your voice and opinion are heard *or* ensure that those less likely to speak feel free to give input?

- make peace *or* break peace?

How is "worldly wisdom" hindering your walk and your readiness for service and/or leadership? In what area(s) do you most need to grow in "true wisdom"? What is your plan to do this? To whom will you be accountable? Write your prayer as a commitment to God.

1. *Spirit-Filled Life Bible* (Nashville: Thomas Nelson Publishers, 1991), 1897, "Word Wealth: James 2:9, show partiality," and margin note on James 2:9.

2. Ibid., 172, Note on Leviticus 19:18. Ibid., 1897, Notes on James 2:8 and 2:10–13.

3. Ibid., 1898, "Word Wealth: James 2:22, working together" and Note on James 2:22.

4. Ibid., 1896, Note on James 1:26, 27.

5. Ibid., 1903, "Truth-In-Action through James."

6. Ralph P. Martin, *James*, Word Biblical Commentary, Vol. 48 (Waco: Word Books, 1988), 129–130. Gerhard Kittel and Gerhard Friedrich, editors, *Theological Dictionary of the New Testament*, Abridged in one volume by Geoffrey W. Bromiley (Grand Rapids: William B. Eerdmans Publishing Company, 1985), *praüs, praütes*, 929–930. Colin Brown, ed., *The New International Dictionary of New Testament Theology*, Vol. 2 (Grand Rapids: Zondervan Publishing House, 1986), 256–259.

Lesson 3/Test: Surrendering the Present and Future to God
(James 4:1—5:20)

Few secular movies have touched my dreams and fears and visualized hope for the future as poignantly as *Mr. Holland's Opus*. Mr. Holland, a talented man whose heart-dream is to compose glorious symphonies, is seemingly turned aside from his destiny by the hard necessities of life. Yet, as he faithfully carries out his tasks each day by continually giving himself more fully to the lot that has been handed him, he weaves his life and gifts into the lives of many others. In the end, the testimony and love of those he has served become the beautiful and unexpected "symphony" he has created—his lasting, living opus.

As James concludes his little book, he continues reaching back to his first message of perseverance and the promise of the crown of life. In chapters 4 and 5, he seems to be offering a word of hope similar to that found in *Mr. Holland's Opus*: the great victory comes by the faithful actions of the day. James challenges us to surrender the present and future to God by: (1) humbly submitting ourselves to God's authority (4:1–12), (2) eradicating prideful presumption (4:13—5:6), (3) fortifying ourselves to persevere (5:7–12), and (4) continuing in loving ministry to one another (5:13–20).

HUMBLY SUBMIT YOURSELF TO GOD (JAMES 4:1–12)

James continues contrasting false and true wisdom or the false and true life of faith. He reveals the ugly facts concerning chronic personal and corporate strife among believers (4:1–5) and spells out the effective solution to all such wars (4:6–10). Then, James offers a specific exhortation concerning interpersonal relationships (4:11, 12).

What seems to be the shape of the strife and disorder among the believers to whom James writes? (4:1, 2a, 11a)

Based on the behaviors described in this and earlier sections of text, what do you think the disorderly covet most? (James 3, especially verses 1 and 14; 4:1–12)

Earlier James wrote that worldly wisdom which leads to disorder and sin is "earthly, sensual, and demonic" (3:14–16). Where does James now lay the responsibility for strife? (4:1, 2)

How could the frustrated, contentious Christians receive what they need from God? (4:2–4)

List the two synonymous labels given these "adulterers." Then, compare their "double-mindedness" with that of the "unwise" described in 1:6–8. (4:4; 1:6–8)

 BIBLE EXTRA

Spiritual Adultery: James's Jewish readers would have quickly recognized the Old Testament metaphor he uses for those who are divided in their affections and commitment to God. Marriage was frequently used as an analogy of God's relationship to Israel. And Israel was often described as "unfaithful" in that she did not consistently love and serve God. As a jealous husband, God yearns for His people's loyalty, trust, and love. God is gracious and patient with His erring bride. Yet unrepentant "adulterers" not only separate themselves from the covenant blessings intended for them but make themselves recipients of God's hostility, chastisement, and the possibility of estrangement from Him (James 4:4–7; Jer. 31:31; Ezek. 16:1–22; Eph. 5:23–32).

James declares that God will give grace and "more grace" which is sufficient to cure worldliness, heal the broken relationship with God which lies at its root, and bring the rule of the Spirit (4:6). In verses 7 through 10, he defines this special favor and unction in terms of specific promises linked to specific actions. Using the guide below, list the actions James commands and the results they will produce.

Verse	Action Commanded	Result Promised
4:7	_____	
	_____ →	_____
4:8a	_____ →	_____
4:8b	_____ →	_____
4:9	_____ →	_____
4:10	_____ →	_____

WORD WEALTH

"**Submit to God . . . Humble yourself**" (James 4:7, 10): The imperatives "humble" and "submit" are close synonyms here. In fact, verse 10 is a reiteration of verse 7. "Humble" (*tapeinoō*, Strong's #5013) means "to make low" and describes a person fully surrendered to God and "devoid of all arrogance and self-exaltation." Similarly, "submit" (*hupotassō*, Strong's #5293) means "to align oneself under" or "to be subservient to" God.

One cannot simply resist Satan and cause him to flee. One must first fully submit to God (4:8, 9). This humbling or submission consists of godly sorrow and confession of sin, which results in a clean, undivided heart. It includes a recommitment to God of all areas of life so that one's hands (activities) are blameless. This humble placement under God is an act of worship which releases God's grace. God draws near, not only enabling the will to refuse Satan's enticements, but also securing the victory as the Christian takes the offensive by resisting Satan with the Word of God (see Luke 4:1–13).

Satan lures us toward defeat by tempting the flesh and will to submit to his ways and use their own strength to get what they want. God calls us to depend on His grace working in and through us as the only way to victory. "The Bible warns that exalting self will lead to a disgraceful fall, but humbling oneself leads to exaltation in this world and the next."[1] The life of peace founded upon humility and submission to God is true wisdom. (3:17, 18; 4:6–10; Prov. 1:7)

What is James's specific exhortation to this strife-prone people? (4:11a)

What law is broken and judged unworthy of obedience when one condemns and slanders a fellow believer? How is this a specific rebellion against God's person and authority? (1:25; 2:8, 12; 4:11, 12)

ERADICATE PRIDEFUL PRESUMPTION (JAMES 4:13—5:6)

This section of text is tied very closely to 4:1–12, for the topic is still adulterous friendship with the world versus life under God's authority and rule. Although James looks at the actions of specific groups (merchants and rich landlords), his warning against prideful presumption applies to all who live in this world and are vulnerable to its distractions.

Why is it foolish for these merchants (or anyone) to ignore God when planning the future? (4:13, 14)

Why is such presumptuous planning a double evil? (4:16, 17)

In your own words, rewrite verse 15 as a principle for life. (4:15; see Prov. 3:6)

Most English Bibles group verse 17 with verses 13–16. How would it also relate to 5:1–6 and the royal law? (3:8; 4:17; 5:1–6)

Material wealth of itself is not evil. Jesus Himself seems to commend skillful acquisition of wealth in the parable of the talents (Matt. 25:14–30). People of faith and godly character like Abraham, Joseph, Lazarus, and Lydia made wise use of wealth. Because their hearts were submitted to God, money and what it could buy was not their source of security, power, or joy. But what is wrong with the way the rich landlords:

obtained their riches? (5:4)

used their wealth? (5:3b, 5)

used the political power derived from wealth? (5:4, 6)

How might riches "eat your flesh like a fire" in this life? Stand as a witness against you in the judgment? (5:3, 5; also Matt. 25:14–30, 31–46)

Who stands in judgment against the arrogant rich who oppress the poor? (5:4)

Word Wealth

The Lord of Sabaoth (James 5:4): The Hebrew title "Lord of *Sabaôth*" is literally "Lord of Hosts." He is the Commander of all the angelic armies, the One mighty in battle who has complete sovereignty and power over heaven and earth. This title declares the complete inability of the self-indulgent rich to evade accountability to God and underlines James's warning that "God resists the proud" (4:6).

Yet the title itself also hints at the great grace and privilege given to the ones who serve God in humility and faith. Psalm 24 shows the "Lord of Hosts" to be also the "King of Glory." This King reveals His glory to those who so desire their full inheritance that they diligently seek His face and stand before Him without hypocrisy. (Ps. 24; also Josh. 5:14; Jer. 31:9)

Faith Alive

Looking at the different groups mentioned in 4:1—5:6, how would you say the status of a believer's relationship with God affects others? Consequently, can your growth in Christ be merely a personal matter? Explain.

What place do you give God in your life? Is He at the helm, on the sidelines, or forgotten? How so?

Where are you most likely to omit God from your plans? In money matters? relationships? life direction/career? the events of the day? What will you do to acknowledge Him as Lord in that area(s)?

What good do you know to do but are neglecting? How will you rectify this fact?

In 4:1–5:6, James reveals God as Husband and Giver of Grace, Lawgiver and Lord, and the mighty Lord of Hosts. Using one of these titles for God, write or speak a word of thanksgiving, praise, and adoration to Him.

FORTIFY YOURSELF TO PERSEVERE (JAMES 5:7–12)

With verse 7, James begins to frame his closing comments with words which recall the promise and hope of the opening section of his epistle. Using examples of the farmer, the prophets, and Job, he affectionately addresses the "brethren," encouraging them to fortify themselves to persevere in faith.

What repeated command points out the main exhortation of verses 7–9? What is the motivation for keeping this command? (5:7–9)

What other commands are given? How are they related to the main exhortation? (5:7–9)

 WORD WEALTH

Be Patient (James 5:7, 8): *Makrothumeō* (Strong's *#3114*), formed from *makros* (long) and *thumos* (temper), is a verb which calls for restraint. It is related to the virtue of longsuffering or forbearance and has to do with enduring delays by holding actions and emotions in check. Thus, *makrothumeō* is closely related to the command "establish [stabilize] your hearts" and the prohibition "do not grumble against one another." Here, "grumble" *(stenazō)* emphasizes emotion and is an unexpressed, inward groaning against a fellow believer.[2]

Earlier James cautioned believers not to slander or condemn a brother (4:11, 12). Here he goes even further, warning believers to hold no bitterness or churning resentment in the heart. What is the double reason behind this caution? (5:9)

 BIBLE EXTRA

Judgment and the Soon-Coming Judge: Read the Scriptures listed below. Then explain why believers must let go of bitter emotions and assumptions, handing all final judgments to the true Judge.

1 Samuel 16:7   Corinthians 4:1–5

1 Chronicles 28:9a   Revelations 2:2a, 23

Jeremiah 17:9, 10   Revelations 14:13

My explanation:

Now read 1 Corinthians 5:1–5, which speaks of judging obvious, outward sin within the Christian community. How would you balance the two messages?

The example of the farmer seems to pertain to the trials and suffering common to every Christian. Farmers must faithfully work and patiently endure all that the physical elements and the natural cycles of seasons may hand them. They must suffer delays and disappointments, overcome distractions, distresses, and irritations, and remain steadfast in the face of the injustice and oppression common to life in a fallen world (5:1–6, 7–9). The message James implies through the example of the farmer is stated succinctly in Galatians 6:9 (which see).

In light of the entire Book of James, how would you identify the "precious fruit" which is harvested by "ordinary Christians" who, like the farmer, patiently persevere?

1:4 _spiritual maturity_   4:6 _____

1:5 _____   4:7 _____

1:12_____   4:8a _____

2:22_____   4:10 _____

3:13_____   5:11 _____

3:17_____   5:16b_____

What action is characteristic of prophets? How does it relate to the type of suffering they must endure? (5:10)

How is patience and restraint called for in the prophets' particular situations? (5:10; see Matt. 5:11, 12 and Heb. 11)

Job is mentioned as an example of one who endures another, different type of trial. Read Job 1:1—2:8. What is the source and character of Job's suffering? (5:11; Job 1:1—2:8)

God did not send the death, destruction, and disease experienced by Job, but He did monitor and allow it. What was the end result of Job's suffering in terms of the spiritual, relational, physical, and material? (5:11; Job 42:1–17)

List the three phrases which describe the way in which Job was unique in his era. (Job 1:1, 8; 2:1; also 2:9, 10)

In light of 1 Corinthians 10:13 and this description, will all suffer the depth of satanic attack that Job endured? Pairing this fact with the truth and provision of 1 Corinthians 10:13 and James 1:5, what is the possibility of success in trials and the temptations they produce? (1:5; 5:11; 1 Cor. 10:13)

What is James's principal admonition for sufferers? How does this admonition reflect a supreme test? (See Job 2:9; 42:7b, 8; Prov. 18:21; James 3:2; 5:12)

     BEHIND THE SCENES

Swearing an Oath: Originally, swearing an oath was an attempt to invoke the character and authority of God in support of one's claim or promise (see: Lev. 19:12; Deut. 23:23). James follows Jesus in prohibiting such a practice (Matt. 5:33–37; James 5:12). Not only does it debase and trivialize the Lord's name and authority, but failure to fully carry out one's oath dishonors God's holiness before the world. Thus, James calls for integrity in speech. This warning is especially important during severe trials when one is tempted to blame God, bargain foolishly, or even defy Him.

James states that anything other than a simple statement of fact or reply causes one to "fall into *hypocrite*" ("theatrical dialogue" or "hypocrisy").[3] If a person's character is above reproach, spoken words do not need to be bolstered by oaths.

CONTINUE IN VIBRANT, LOVING MINISTRY TO ONE ANOTHER (JAMES 5:13–20)

Here, James brings his final remarks to a close. He has assured his readers that there is a positive side to adversity. He has shown that if one is in the midst of a trial, there is help in God. Now, James strongly pronounces God to be the answer for every situation and circumstance of life. He declares that

God's provisions to and through His people are more than enough for every need. James gives specific directives concerning situations which commonly confront the church as he expounds the miraculous power of prayer and the mighty power of watchful mutual care.

List the two situations mentioned in verses 13 and 14. Then, describe their solutions in light of present and previous texts.

1.   (1:5; 5:13)

2.   (1:2, 3; 5:13)

What directives are given for physical healing in the church? Who is to initiate the process? Administrate on behalf of the church? What are the elements of this ministry? (5:14, 15)

BIBLE EXTRA

The Preparation and Healing Ministry of Elders: Elders are a special group of officers in the local church who are to meet specific criteria (1 Tim. 3:1–7; Titus 1:5–9). Not only are they to be upright in lifestyle and mature in Christ, these particular elders must move in discernment (James 5:15, 16) and the gift of faith (1 Cor. 12:9). Such elders should also be fully prepared in their private prayer life (see Matt. 6:6) and earnest and fervent in prayer and faith on behalf of the sick (James 4:2, 3; 5:16).

It is the elders' faith-filled prayer which ministers miraculous physical restoration. This type of prayer is offered in the name and character of Jesus (John 16:23, 24) and appropriated through the power of the Holy Spirit, whose presence is symbolized by the anointing oil (James 5:14).

Although other means of miraculous physical healing are recorded in early church history and can be verified today, this ministry is the customary provision for healing in the local congregation. For this reason, James 5:13–15 is often called "The Divine Healing Covenant of the New Testament" and related to Exodus 15:22–27, which records the divine healing covenant of the Old Testament.[4]

Verse 15 shows that confession of sin will, at times, be part of the healing ministry of elders. The verb used to describe the action indicates an ongoing pattern of sinning. How might ongoing, willful sin be the root of sickness? What is James's remedy to prevent sin from becoming entrenched in the believer's life and leading to illness or death? (5:16; see also Prov. 28:13)

 PROBING THE DEPTHS

A rule for confession of sin might be: (1) **Private sin** needs to be confessed in a private setting before a godly intercessor, a Christian counselor, or an accountability group with which one is in covenant. (2) **Public sin** (sin which is known or visible and directly detrimental to the church community) needs to be confessed publicly. Where possible and helpful, apology and retribution should be made. Where needed, new boundaries should be set and accountability obtained to prevent falling into the same sin in the future. In all cases, the life should be re-formed and strengthened by pertinent topical study of the Scripture and the establishment of daily devotions (see Lesson 9: "Overcoming Sin Habits").

Read James 5:16b–18 and the account to which this passage refers. Describe the power and effectiveness of Elijah's prayers and the manner in which he prayed. (1 Kin. 17:1–7; 18:1, 41–46; James 5:16b–18)

What encouragement does James offer based on this account? (5:16b, 17a) How is this encouragement related to the practice of confessing trespasses to one another? (5:16; see also Matt. 5:23, 24)

Bring together what you have learned in James about prayer; use it to describe "effective, fervent prayer" and "the righteous person" who would offer such a prayer. (You may wish to jot down the facts under these headings.)

Effective, Fervent Prayer   *The Righteous Petitioner*

Throughout the Book of James we have seen how Christians might drift from the foundation of faith in their beliefs or lifestyle. What elements might be involved in facilitating the "turning" or repentance of a fellow believer? What will these loving acts accomplish? (5:19, 20)

FAITH ALIVE

How has the Holy Spirit spoken to your heart as you have studied the closing passages of James (5:7–12, 13–20)? What commitment are you willing to make based on this conviction? How will you begin this week?

What particular challenge and encouragement have you received from James 4:1—5:20 which will help you more completely surrender your present and future to the Lord?

Scan through the Faith Alive sections you have completed in your study of the Book of James. How have you kept
your commitments to put faith into action? On which one(s)
will you continue to concentrate as you leave the study of
James?

1. *Spirit-Filled Life Bible* (Nashville: Thomas Nelson Publishers, 1991), 1439, "Word
Wealth: Matt. 18:4, humbles." Ibid., 1742, "Word Wealth: 1 Cor. 14:32, subject." Ibid.,
1900, "Word Wealth: James 4:10, lift up."
2. Ibid., 1878, "Word Wealth: Heb. 6:12, patience." Fritz Rienecker and Cleon
Rogers, *Linguistic Key to the Greek New Testament* (Grand Rapids: Zondervan Publishing
House, 1980), 740.
3. *Spirit-Filled Life Bible*, 1901, Note on James 5:12. Ibid., 1775, "Word Wealth: Gal.
2:13, hypocrite."
4. Ibid., 1901, Notes on James 5:14 and James 5:15. Ibid., 1901–1902, "Kingdom
Dynamics: James 5:13–18, The New Testament Divine Healing Covenant."

Lesson 4/ Test: Maintaining a Living Hope in Times of Suffering
(1 Pet. 1:1—2:10)

The ragtag band of prisoners, exiled hundreds of miles from their homeland, worked as slaves for their captors. Day and night, they carried out their menial and grueling tasks—scrubbing wooden floors, carrying heavy loads of water and wood, digging the clay pits, chopping weeds, and harvesting the crops they set on their masters' tables. As months became years, their heads and hearts and demeanors lowered until they walked bowed at the shoulders, eyes to the ground.

All, that is, except one young girl, barely fourteen years of age. Each week her shoulders grew straighter. Each year she held herself with new dignity and grace. She fulfilled her duties with graciousness, poise, and skill despite the lowly tasks which occupied her day or the slave uniform which she wore. When asked why she was so pleasant to her hateful captors and why she acted as though she were not a slave at all, she replied: "I am the daughter of the great King Tigius. Since the day I was born, I have been betrothed to Prince Biaigus who ascends the throne. Though I wear the clothes of the lowest slave, I know who I am and I know the destiny to which I was born. Dear Biaigus will soon come, and King Tigius shall stand on the hill as the Prince takes all these under his domain. I have pledged myself to always be what I am. Any day now I shall return home, and I will do so with the nobility and honor of my father's name."

Similarly, in the first chapters of his first epistle, the apostle Peter points us toward home, focusing our attention not on the hardships we may encounter but the great destiny and hope to which we have been born. He encourages us to live above present circumstances and maintain a living hope in times of suffering, for our salvation is about to be revealed.

OVERVIEW OF 1 PETER

Before you begin the first lesson in 1 Peter, do a quick reading of the entire epistle. Notice the tone or mood of the book. Jot down frequently repeated words and phrases and any pressing questions you would like to answer during your study. When you have finished, answer the questions below, and study the information in the chart.

James and Peter both speak to Christians going through adversity, yet the tone of the two letters is decidedly different. How do you account for the mood of 1 Peter in terms of the book's main message and its particular readers?

The epistle clearly states that the apostle Peter is its author and that Silvanus (Silas) likely acted as secretary in its composition (1:1; 5:12). We learn from the Gospels that Peter was a strong, assertive leader with a dominant personality. Read the passages listed below which offer a few vignettes of Peter's early days with Jesus. Then, tell how the fact of Peter's authorship of a book about humble submission and joy in times of suffering is both a testimony and an encouragement to you. (Jesus rebukes Peter: Matt. 16:21–23; the transfiguration account: Matt. 17:1–4; cutting off the priest's ear: Luke 22:47–51 and John 18:10, 11)

AT A GLANCE

THE FIRST EPISTLE OF PETER

Date and Place of Writing

First Peter was most likely written in Rome during the early A.D. 60s just before A.D. 64/65 when Nero began severely persecuting the Christians in Rome. Ancient tradition holds that the apostle Peter was martyred during Nero's purge.[1]

The Letter's Recipients

The Pilgrims of the Dispersion residing in Pontus, Galatia, Cappadocia, Asia, and Bithynia (1:1) were mostly Gentile converts to Christianity whom Peter addresses as Jews in light of their status as "chosen people" and "sojourners" in this world. It is likely they became Christians following the outpouring of the Spirit on the Day of Pentecost or during a non-Pauline evangelism campaign.[2]

REJOICE! YOU HAVE BEEN BORN INTO A GREAT AND LIVING HOPE! (1 PET. 1:1–12)

With the exuberant joy of one whose eyes have seen beyond the finish line, Peter describes the salvation about to be revealed. He recounts the election (1:1, 2), the great present hope (1:3–9), and the high privilege (1:10–12) into which the saints of Asia Minor and we ourselves have entered.

How does Peter describe the work of each Person of the Trinity in our salvation? What is the human part in the work of salvation? (1:2; see Ex. 24:4–8)

 AT A GLANCE

THE TRINITY AT WORK IN SALVATION[3]
Elected by foreknowledge: Just as the nation Israel was selected in eternity past, God the Father chose the church and us individually as His own people.
Sanctified: In time, we were set apart to God by the work of the Holy Spirit, who led us to repentance, so that we believed the truth of the gospel and yielded our obedience to God.
Sprinkled with Jesus' blood: By the work of Jesus, we were brought into covenant relationship with God and received the benefits of the blood of Christ in forgiveness, justification, redemption, and salvation.

What Person of the Trinity is emphasized in verses 3–5? Based on these verses, what praise will you offer Him for who He is and what He has done? (1:3)

How would you define the present "living hope" into which Christians have been born? What is the basis and power of this "living hope"? (1:3)

WORD WEALTH

Hope (1 Pet. 1:3): *elpis* (Strong's *#1680*), is not an optimistic outlook or wishful thinking which has no foundation. It is a "confident expectation based on solid certainty. Biblical hope rests on God's promises, particularly those pertaining to Christ's return. So certain is the future of the redeemed that the NT sometimes speaks of future events in the past tense, as though they were already accomplished. Hope is never inferior to faith, but it is an extension of faith. Faith is the present possession of grace; hope is confidence in grace's future accomplishment." [4]

What, in our salvation, is yet to come? (1:4; Rev. 21:1— 22:17)

BIBLE EXTRA

An Inheritance in Heaven (1 Pet. 1:4): Scripture shows that those who belong to Christ are made joint heirs together with Him (Rom. 8:15–17). This privilege means that believers become not only partakers of Jesus' resurrection life, but also participants in His rule and citizens of the New Jerusalem and the heavens and earth which are to come (Rom. 8:19, 21; Heb. 11:10, 16; 12:22; 13:14; 2 Pet. 3:13; Rev. 21 and 22). This high honor, however, requires sincere and living faith. Scripture clearly shows that those who suffer with Christ will partake in His glory and His reign and that reward and inheritance are related to faithfulness and Christlikeness (Matt. 25:34; Rom. 8:17b; Phil. 3:10; 2 Tim. 2:12). [5]

In this present world, everything is vulnerable to death, loss, and deterioration. What guarantees assure that we will indeed receive our heavenly inheritance?
Guarantee #1 (1:4)

Guarantee #2 (1:4)

Guarantee #3 (1:5)

WORD WEALTH

Kept by the power of God (1 Pet. 1:5): *Phroureō* (Strong's *#5432*), meaning "shielded," "protected" or "kept," is a military term which pictures "a sentry standing guard as protection against the enemy." As Christians, we know that we are in continual spiritual combat in this world. But we can proceed with confidence since it is not our strength but God's power (1:5) and God's peace (Phil. 4:7) which shield and keep us.[6]

James and Peter both urge believers to rejoice in adversity. They both see trials as necessary. How do their reasons differ? How are they similar? Which offers you the most motivation? Why? (James 1:2–4; 1 Pet. 1:6, 7)

How is it possible that a person can be both distressed and rejoicing? What biblical character or personal acquaintance best exemplifies this hope-filled life to you? (1:6, 7)

PROBING THE DEPTHS

The One-Hundred-Year Test: If Peter were alive in modern times, he might put his stamp of approval on "the one-hundred-year test." When immersed in the depths of adversity which threatens to overwhelm you with anxiety or distress, ask yourself: What significance will this situation bear one hundred years from now? What significance will my response to it have in one hundred years? This simple test has a way of quickly putting everything in the correct perspective!

What three actions or qualities characterize the present life of genuine faith? How descriptive are these of your life? (1:8, 9)

The salvation made available to us through Christ has little appeal for many today. Even Christians are sometimes lax in searching the Scriptures to know the wonders and benefits which are freely ours in Christ. Why would the disclosures of verses 10–12 help encourage sufferers in the pursuit of God? How do they encourage you?

 FAITH ALIVE

Peter emphasizes the wonder and glory of a salvation to be received in the future. How is the "living hope" and the "inheritance . . . reserved in heaven for you" affecting your attachments, goals, priorities, and values in this world today? What, if anything, needs to change?

What idea or understanding from 1 Peter 1:1–12 will be the most helpful to you when you enter a trial which tests your faith? Select a verse to memorize which will become part of your "arsenal" against the accusations and temptations of Satan.

OFFER THE APPROPRIATE RESPONSE OF A LIFE OF HOLINESS AND LOVE (1 PET. 1:13—2:3)

If you've ever moved away from a permanent residence to a short-term location, you know that you live in a temporary residence in a different way. You don't join the community groups or get too deeply involved in local issues. You don't change wallpaper, invest in the picture that is "just right" for the living room, or purchase the small but expensive knick-knacks which add the finishing touches to your home. Every purchase, every investment of money, time, or energy is weighed in light of whether it will benefit the place of your permanent residence. Your heart and focus is somewhere else.

In 1 Peter 1:1–12, the apostle made it clear that the fulfillment of our great hope resides "ahead of us" and that our attachment to this present life is tentative. Now, Peter shows that when our heart and focus is on our heavenly inheritance, the appropriate lifestyle is one of holiness and full separation unto God.

List the six commands Peter issues in verses 13 through 17. Then, using your own words, tell what each means.

1.   (1:13a)

2.   (1:13b)

3.   (1:13c)

4.   (1:14; see Rom. 12:2)

5.   (1:15)

6.   (1:17b)

 BEHIND THE SCENES

Gird up: During the Old Testament and early New Testament eras, to "gird up" had special meaning based on the culture and dress of the time. Since all wore long robelike clothing, it was very difficult to move freely when special exertion, speed, or agility was called for, as when one must run or fight. Thus, one would pull up his robe and belt it. The resulting short tunic would facilitate the accomplishment of the task at hand.

"Gird up the loins of your mind" is a call to alertness and readiness of will, spiritual attitude, and mental faculties. In a sense, Peter says: "Get ready to run with all that is in you!" [7]

What is the first reason offered by Peter for commanding these actions? (1:16)

 WORD WEALTH

Holy (1 Pet. 1:15, 16), *hagios* (Strong's *#40*), means "consecrated to God," "pure" or "blameless," "separated" or "marked out for God." It describes God in that He is separate from the created order and the world system in person and character. The command "become holy" calls us to display the family likeness and prepare ourselves for heaven, in which is no unholiness. This work of "holiness" or "sanctification" is performed by the Holy Spirit as one yields to Him in His personal dealings and in the diligent study of Scripture. (See: 1 Pet. 1:2; 1:22—2:3; John 17:16–19.)

What is the second reason for Peter's commands? (1:17a)

How would you bring together the two diverse images of "Father" and "Judge" to describe the relationship and action suggested in verse 17?

What is the third reason for Peter's six commands? (1:18–21)

From what "aimless conduct" have you been redeemed? In other words, what is your testimony of the transforming action of Christ in your life which has separated you from your old ways and former heritage? (1:18)

 BEHIND THE SCENES

Redemption: Redemption is an Old Testament concept seen in the role of the kinsman-redeemer who would recover for a close relative the property, family inheritance, and status which had been lost through poverty, helplessness, or violence. This redeemer paid a price which was so far beyond the reach of the kinsman as to be utterly impossible for him to pay.

In the same sense, Jesus has redeemed us from sin and death and recovered our lost inheritance. The price was the blood of His sinless life of full obedience which was offered on our behalf. The great love of God and the high value He places on human life is clearly seen in His willingness to surrender His Son, who was the only adequate substitutionary sacrifice.

Peter states that the high price of our salvation is not a thing to be taken lightly. Rather, the awareness of it should affect every dimension of our lives. (See Lev. 25:23–25, 47–49; Ruth 2—4; Ps. 72:14; Isa. 52:9; Jer. 32:6–11; Rom. 8:20–23.)[8]

How is God's love seen in the fact that Jesus' redeeming work was "foreordained before the foundation of the world"? Take time to thank God for His boundless love. (1:20, 21)

What human act begins the process of holiness in the Christian's life? Through what two divine agents is it begun and carried out? (1:22–25)

How is the human will involved in the ongoing process? What two opposite actions are required? (2:1, 2)

How does the willful "laying aside" of evil and taking in God's Word prove one's initial salvation and the fact of one's eternal inheritance? (2:3)

What is the supreme manifestation of holiness and the denial of "all malice, all deceit, hypocrisy, envy, and all evil speaking"? (1:22; 2:1)

WORD WEALTH

Sincere love of the brethren (1:22): "Sincere," *anupokritos* (Strong's *#505*) means "without hypocrisy" or "devoid of any pretension." Peter shows that such sincere love is "fervent" (done with a zeal which pushes one to the highest level of performance) and "pure" (unpolluted, clean, and fully ethical).[9]

FAITH ALIVE

Are you living the Christian life as a "world citizen," an "alien without a green card," or a "big-time landlord"? How can you prove this?

How would you honestly assess your "love-level" and your "milk-hunger"? Growing? Satisfied? Not even on the scale? What do you need to ask God to help you do? What is your part?

Do you most need to "gird up your mind," "set your hope fully on heaven," "be self-controlled," "stop conforming to the old life," or "become holy"? What steps will you take to do this?

For what fellow believer do you need to develop a sincere love? Ask God for the help of the Holy Spirit. Then begin to pray for that person's blessing, growth, and prosperity. Look for ways to demonstrate love.

RECOGNIZE YOUR GLORIOUS NEW IDENTITY AND STATUS IN CHRIST (1 PET. 2:4–10)

Having pointed suffering Christians toward their soon-coming inheritance, and having urged them to live with new determination a life of holiness and love, Peter returns to an opening topic. He discusses just what election by God means in this life. Peter challenges us to recognize the glorious new identity and status we have in Christ today.

Read verses 4–10. What seems to be the key word of the entire section? How was this word/idea used in the opening of chapter 1? (1:2; 2:4–10)

     WORD WEALTH

"**Chosen,**" *eklektos* (Strong's *#1588*) is used in one of its forms in 1 Peter 1:1; 2:4, 6, 9. It comes from *ek,* "out of" and *lego,* "to select, to gather" and indicates "one picked out

or gathered from among the larger group for special service
or privilege." It is used in Luke to describe Jesus as Messiah
(23:35) and elsewhere to describe Christians as recipients of
the special favor of God (Matt. 24:22; Rom. 8:33; Col. 3:12).
In 1 Peter 2:4–10, the term is used in close conjunction with
"precious." The high value affixed to the "elected" is derived
from their attachment to Jesus, the Chosen and the Precious
of the Father (1 Pet. 2:4).[10]

Peter identifies Jesus as "the living stone" and further as
the cornerstone or capstone—a massive, foundational stone
around which the walls of a building are joined or the center
stone which gives an arch its stability. How can this metaphor
be related to Jesus and the church? (2:2–7)

To God and believers the cornerstone is precious (2:4, 7).
How do unbelievers respond to Jesus? (2:4, 7, 8)

WORD WEALTH

"Rejected" (1 Pet. 2:4, 7), from *apodokimazō* (Strong's
#593), means "to refuse after examination" or "to examine
and reckon of little value." These rejecters are disobedient to
the truth concerning Jesus (1 Pet. 2:7, 8). Having refused to
believe, they have no spiritual eyes to see the things of the
kingdom (John 3:3). Thus, they continue on their path of
destruction and fulfill their unchanged destiny (2:8). In contrast to believers who will "by no means be put to shame,"
their rejection of Christ will cause their fall, for their house will
utterly crumble (2:5, 6, 8).[11]

What does being "as living stones" mean in the Christian's relationship to God? to other believers? to unbelievers?
(2:4–10)

List the identity and status given to believers in Christ. Think about what each means to you. (2:5, 9, 10)

What two services are believers to perform in light of this wonderful status and identity? (2:5b, 9b, 10)

BIBLE EXTRA

The Priority of Worship: "As a 'royal' priesthood, the kingly nature of the redeemed worshiper is noted. This passage is rooted in God's call to ancient Israel (see Ex. 19:5–7). Peter and John (Rev. 1:5, 6) draw this truth to full application and prophetic fulfillment in the NT believer. As with Israel, deliverance through the blood of the Lamb is but the beginning. As promised, dominion and destiny will unfold as their priestly duty is fulfilled. True authority is always related to a walk in purity and a constancy in worship. The spirit of worship is essential to all advance of the kingdom. Just as ancient Israel will only take the Promised Land while doing battle from a foundation of righteous worship before the Lord, so with the contemporary church. We will only experience promised power for evangelism and spiritual victories as we prioritize and grow in our worship of the living God. Kingdom power is kept from pollution this way, as kingdom people keep humbly praiseful before the King—and witness His works of power with joy" (see Rev. 1:5, 6; Dan. 7:21, 22).[12]

FAITH ALIVE

How do you feel about being "chosen," "holy," and "a special people" of God? When is it the most difficult for you to remember these truths about your identity and status? You may want to memorize 1 Peter 2:9, 10.

Where has your "darkness" been turned to "light," and how has God's mercy been especially extended to you? Take time to thank and praise God.

First Peter 1:1—2:10 shows that "the chosen" also choose God and the true life of worship. Where would you say you are today in offering the spiritual sacrifices of thanksgiving, praise, and adoration as a way of life? What will you do?

1. *Spirit-Filled Life Bible* (Nashville: Thomas Nelson, 1991), 1905, Introduction to the First Epistle of Peter.

2. Ibid., 1907, map entitled "A Letter to Christians Abroad." Also, J. Ramsey Michaels, *1 Peter*, Word Biblical Commentary (Waco: Word Books, 1988), 49:8–9.

3. *Spirit-Filled Life Bible*, 1907, Note on 1 Peter 1:2. William MacDonald, *The Believer's Bible Commentary* (Nashville: Thomas Nelson Publishers, 1995), 2250.

4. *Spirit-Filled Life Bible*, 1826, "Word Wealth: 1 Thess. 1:3, hope."

5. *Nelson's Illustrated Bible Dictionary* (Nashville: Thomas Nelson Publishers, 1986), 467, 507.

6. *Spirit-Filled Life Bible*, 1907, "Word Wealth: 1 Pet. 1:5, kept."

7. Fritz Rienecker and Cleon Rogers, *Linguistic Key to the Greek New Testament* (Grand Rapids: Zondervan Publishing House, 1980), 747.

8. *Spirit-Filled Life Bible*, 1031, "Word Wealth, Is. 52:9." Ibid., 1908, "Kingdom Dynamics: 1 Pet. 1:18, 19, Man's Greatest Need Is for Salvation."

9. Ibid., 1909, "Word Wealth: 1 Pet. 1:22, sincere." Ibid., 1411, "Word Wealth: Matt. 5:8, pure." Rienecker and Rogers, *Linguistic Key*, 749.

10. *Spirit-Filled Life Bible*, 1910, "Word Wealth: 1 Pet. 2:9, chosen."

11. Rienecker and Rogers, *Linguistic Key*, 750.

12. *Spirit-Filled Life Bible*, 1910, "Kingdom Dynamics: 1 Pet. 2:9, Priority of Worship."

Lesson 5/Test: Leading an Exemplary Life in Difficult Times and Trying Relationships
(1 Pet. 2:11—5:14)

It has been many years now, but his memories are clear. A third imprisonment for preaching the good news. A transfer from crowded cell to labor camp. An assignment which amounted to a signed death warrant.

In the beginning, the stench of the cesspool had left him reeling with nausea, weak, and trembling. But as Pastor Chen stood alone raking the human waste which swirled around him and calling upon the name of his Jesus, the answer came. Even more tangibly than during the proclamation of the gospel, he could sense the Lord saying: "You are My own."

The affliction prescribed by his enemies to break his body and his faith became the place of Pastor Chen's breakthrough into the heavenlies—his private garden. The sweet fragrance of his praise was echoed by the sweet presence of his Lord, and all was well. To this day, the testimony of George Chen's faith and his Lord's faithfulness remains a witness to all who hear.[1]

Even though statistics show that persecution and violence against Christians is at an all-time high worldwide, few who read this account will suffer similar adversity. Yet, in many ways, we all must be ready and able to present a godly witness during difficult times and in trying relationships. In the context of persecution and suffering, Isaiah declared, "Here am I and the children whom the Lord has given me! We are for signs and wonders in Israel." (Is. 8:18). In 2:11—5:14, Peter affirms the powerful potential of an exemplary life and gives practical advice to help us: (1) live in harmony and submission to all earthly authorities (2:11—3:7), (2) follow Christ's example when suffering because of good works or our Christian faith (3:8—4:19), and (3) serve in the church with humility and wisdom (5:1-14).

LIVE IN HARMONY AND SUBMISSION TO ALL EARTHLY AUTHORITIES (1 PET. 2:11—3:7)

Before talking to specific groups of Christians (citizens, servants, wives, and husbands), Peter offers an introduction to his topic of submission (2:11, 12). He draws his readers' attention back to the fact that they are "sojourners" and "pilgrims" in this world (1:1). It is as if he were saying, "Don't give undue weight to your present, temporary circumstances." He challenges Christians to move their focus away from their particular situation (with its questions of justice, rights, and freedoms) and center it upon the Christian response which will bear eternal significance.

Read 1 Peter 2:11—3:7. What one verse seems to encapsulate the directives for all relationships?

How likely is it that Christians will be criticized by non-Christians? What present and final witnesses will determine the truth concerning your life? (2:12, 15)

Where is the real site of the battle for submission and a godly witness? (2:11)

What is Peter's command and the motivation behind it concerning civil authorities? What groups today might be included in Peter's list? (2:13–16; also see Rom. 13:1–10)

 WORD WEALTH

Free . . . but as bondservants (2:16): Peter's whole idea of submission may be summed up here. As individuals, we are free (*eleutheros,* Strong's *#1658*), "not under legal obligation, freeborn, able to move on our own and come and go as we please." But as Christians, we willfully exchange our independence for servanthood (*doulos,* "slavery" Strong's *#1401*) under God and the authorities He sets (2:14, 16). By doing so, we become "free to serve the Lord in all the ways that are consistent with His word, will, nature, and holiness." [2]

Peter shows that a "master's" or employer's actions are not the determining factor for our responses and actions. What two measures may be used to determine what is commendable on our part? (2:18–20)

Read verses 21–25. Who is the prototype of suffering and righteousness?

 WORD WEALTH

Christ, our Example (2:21): "Example," *hupogrammos* (Strong's *#5261*) derives from *hupo,* "under," and *grapho,* "to write" and originally referred to tracing the letters or copying the handwriting of one's teacher. [3]

Study Jesus' example and list actions restrained and undertaken. (2:22, 23)

Actions Restrained   **The Action Undertaken**

_____   _____

_____   _____

_____   _____

_____   _____

BIBLE EXTRA

The Suffering Servant (2:22–25): Peter quotes a familiar Old Testament passage which would cause his first readers to recall Isaiah's "Suffering Servant" motif with its list of the benefits of salvation. Read Isaiah 53 which lies behind this text. Peter emphasizes Christian conversion as enablement to endure suffering righteously. Not only are Christians dead to sin and alive to righteousness, healing and health has been provided for mind, body, soul, and spirit. (Is. 53; 1 Pet. 2:22–25)[4]

Read 3:1–7. By use of the term "likewise" or "in the same manner," Peter connects the directives to wives and husbands to the servanthood and submission described earlier (2:11–25; 3:1, 7). When talking to wives, how does Peter describe the way in which they should relate to their husbands in:

attitude? (3:2)

action? (3:1, 2, 6)

manner? (3:3–5)

Peter commands "fear" (respect) but warns against being "afraid with any terror" because fear can cause one to act/ react in a nonconstructive or even destructive manner. How could a wife retain her personhood and even disagree with her husband without giving up Peter's directives concerning attitude, action, and manner? (3:6)

 BIBLE EXTRA

Bible Wisdom Concerning Wives and Women: "The spirit of submission, whereby a woman voluntarily acknowledges her husband's leadership responsibility under God, is an act of faith. The Bible nowhere 'submits' or subordinates women to men, generically. But this text calls a woman to submit herself to her husband (Eph. 5:22), and the husband is charged to lovingly give himself to caring for his wife—never exploiting the trust of her submission (v. 7; Eph. 5:25–29). This divinely ordered arrangement is never shown, nor was it ever given, to reduce the potential, purpose, or fulfillment of the woman. Only fallen nature or persistent church traditionalism, finding occasion through 'proof-texts' separated from their full biblical context, can make a case for the social exploitation of women or the restriction of women from church ministry.

"First Timothy 2:12 and 1 Corinthians 14:34, 35, which disallow a woman's teaching (in an unwelcomed manner), usurping authority, or creating a nuisance by public argument, all relate to the woman's relationship with her husband.

"The Bible's word of wisdom to women seems to be summarized in Peter's word here: counsel given to a woman whose husband is an unbeliever. She is told that her 'words' are not her key to success in winning her husband to Christ; but her Christlike, loving spirit is. Similarly, this wisdom would apply to any woman with the potential for a public ministry of leadership in the church. Her place will most likely be given when she is not argumentatively insistent upon it, so much as given to 'winning' it by a gracious, loving, servantlike spirit—the same spirit that ought to be evident in the life of a man who would lead."[5]

What two understandings or "honorings" are foundational to a husband's right relationship with his wife? (3:7)

Understanding that his wife is physically weaker calls a husband to a protective role—an honoring of the way God created women. List practical ways a husband could show consideration for his wife based on this knowledge.

How would a husband honor a wife's spiritual status?

WORD WEALTH

Heirs together of the grace of life (3:7): Here, "fellow heirs of eternal life" is the primary meaning and indicates the full status and inheritance of each spouse in Christ. Yet Peter also may be suggesting that husbands understand that Christian marriage itself is a gracious gift intended to bring a special abundance to this life.

What powerful personal and joint ministry is thwarted when husbands do not dwell with their wives with understanding?

BIBLE EXTRA

Submission and Ethics (2:11—3:7): Peter calls us to obey and respect all authorities. However, not all authorities are godly or ethical. Read Psalm 1:1, 2 and Matthew 22:37–40. How do these laws of relationship and blessing help to weigh the authority of Scripture and conscience against the authority of a supervisor, civil official, or spouse when an ethical issue is at stake?

FAITH ALIVE

What is the context of your greatest battle in regard to submission to authority? What does biblical submission call you to change? How will you go about this?

Describe a marriage of mutual respect in which both partners are fully submitted to God. What qualities from this ideal would you like to see worked into your marriage or dating relationship?

FOLLOW CHRIST'S EXAMPLE WHEN SUFFERING BECAUSE OF GOOD WORKS OR THE CHRISTIAN FAITH (1 PET. 3:8—4:19)

Having addressed specific relational situations affecting individual lives, Peter now broadens his focus and discusses what it means to be a member of the community of faith in times of persecution. Peter talks to the church as a whole as he addresses the topic of suffering which occurs because one lives in this world as a Christian. Read 3:8—4:19.

Why is unity especially important among Christians during times of persecution? What other attitudes should characterize both our life with other Christians and our response when persecuted by unbelievers? (3:8)

How and why should we bless those who insult and persecute us for our faith? (3:9–14a)

What fears probably motivate the persecutors' insults? (3:14b)

What three actions are an antidote for our fear when suffering for doing good? Explain, in practical terms, what each of these means. (3:15–17)

1.

2.

3.

What encouragement is offered sufferers by the story of Noah and the Flood? (3:18–22)

PROBING THE DEPTHS

He preached to spirits in prison (3:18–20): This passage, although probably easily understood by its first readers, is difficult to interpret. It likely refers to the event of Christ's resurrection which openly proclaimed His victory to "spirits in prison"—the demonic spirits behind the corruption of Noah's day (v. 19; see Gen. 6:1–8; 2 Pet. 2:4, 5; Jude 6). Such proclamation may have been an integral part of subjecting "angels and authorities and powers" to Christ's rule (v. 22). A second chance for salvation after this life is not in keeping with Jesus' or apostolic teaching and should not be inferred here.[6]

What is the great benefit of following Christ's example when enduring persecution? (4:1, 2)

For what do unbelievers often ridicule Christians? Why? (4:3, 4)

Read and compare 4:5, 6 with 3:12. Peter says that everyone will be judged according to what they did with the gospel in this flesh-life. What does he show to be the potential of the gospel which is preached by a Christian's life?

What three things does Peter call us to do in light of the times? (4:7)

What is Peter saying about the generosity, character, and power with which we are to minister our gifts—especially love—to the body of Christ? How would you evaluate your service using these three criteria? (4:8–11)

What is the likelihood of "fiery trials"? What double reason for rejoicing does Peter see in them? (4:12, 13)

How can you know that you are suffering "as a Christian"? (4:14–16)

Why is it a gracious act of God for judgment to begin with the family of God? (4:17–19; also 4:1, 2)

 PROBING THE DEPTHS

Christian Persecution and the Great Judgment:
Today we are experiencing a worldwide increase in Christian persecutions, especially in the East. Yet even in nations

where open, violent persecution is not prevalent, it seems the holy lifestyle and the precepts of Christianity are being publicly ridiculed and politically maligned. According to Peter, we should see these facts as an indication that the appointed time for judgment has begun. Instead of complaining or rebelling against God, we should commit ourselves to God and allow suffering to have its full purifying effect on us individually and as a corporate church.

The judgment which begins with the church will culminate in the great outpouring of God's wrath upon unbelievers. For us, judgment brings hope and preparation for Christ's return. For unbelievers, it brings utter hopelessness. (See: Joel 3:9–17; Mal. 3:1–3; 4:1–6; Pet. 4:1, 2, 16–19.)

SERVE IN THE CHURCH WITH HUMILITY AND WISDOM (1 PET. 5:1–14)

Peter pens his exhortations to leaders and members of the church on the heels of his declaration that judgment has begun in the house of God. This context gives added weight to his specific instructions as he urges elders (5:1–4) and all members (5:5–11) to indeed commit their souls to Him in doing good. Read 5:1–14.

Why are wise leadership, humility, and spiritual warfare especially important during times of persecution? (5:1–10)

What attitude and example is Peter trying to communicate by identifying himself as "fellow elder" and "fellow witness"? (5:1; see John 21:15–17)

Contrast each wrong motive/action with the right motive/action for leadership. (5:2, 3)

1.

2.

3.

How/why might leaders be vulnerable to sin in the areas of: satisfaction with their role, money, control, being an example to the flock? How can members help leaders keep right motives in these areas?

 BIBLE EXTRA

Shepherd Leaders (optional): Read the following passages which depict leaders as shepherds and the Lord as the Great Shepherd. Jot down the characteristics of a true shepherd and the tasks a shepherd performs. Decide what each means in practical terms. (Ps. 23; Jer. 3:15; 10:31; Ezek. 34:2–16)

What actions does Peter call for among the membership of the local assemblies? What would obedience to his commands look like in the church's daily life? (5:5, 6)

Compare James's "Submit . . . resist" passage on spiritual warfare with Peter's instruction here. How is submission defined differently in 1 Peter? Is this a contradiction? Why/why not? (5:5–10; James 4:6–10, Lesson 2)

What particular cares or anxieties might plague Peter's first readers or any under the threat of severe persecution? What is the cure? (5:6, 7)

 WORD WEALTH

Casting all your care (5:7): The phrase follows "humble yourselves under the mighty hand of God" and is very closely connected to it. Humble submission brings one under God's protection and grace in a special way. Here, "care," *merimna* (Strong's *#3308,* from *merizō*: "to divide" and *nous*: "the mind") denotes distracting "anxieties," "burdens," or "worries," over daily matters or needs before they arise. We are called "to throw" cares onto God's broad shoulders because His protective and attentive love is well able to secure all our needed provisions.[7]

What personal traits and understandings might be needed to successfully stand against the devil as he is described here? (5:8, 9)

How does the fact of other Christians' suffering serve to encourage faith and perseverance? (5:9)

List the four things God will accomplish in you through suffering. Then tell what each means to you. (5:10)

1.

2.

3.

4.

Note the terms "our faithful brother," "Mark my son," "greet . . . with a kiss of love," and "elect together with you," which are part of the close of Peter's letter. Add the fact that Mark and Silvanus ministered at different times with both Paul and Peter. What observations might be made about life in the early church? (5:12–14)

 BEHIND THE SCENES (optional)

It seems that Silvanus (Silas) and Mark both began their ministries from the Jerusalem church where Peter was one of the early leaders. Both served under Peter at some point. Church tradition holds that Mark ministered in Rome with the apostle Peter during Peter's last years of ministry and that Mark's Gospel is largely based on Peter's preaching.[8] Trace Mark and Silvanus's ministry through the Scripture.

Silvanus (Silas)
Acts 15:22, 32, 40
2 Cor. 1:19
1 Thess. 1:1
2 Thess. 1:1, 2

(John) Mark
Acts 12:12–18, 25; 13:13; 15:36–39
Col. 4:10
Phil. 2:4; 2 Tim. 4:11
Read the Gospel of Mark

 FAITH ALIVE

What area of your life needs to be repaired, established, strengthened, or made steadfast? Surrender that area to God. Ask Him to begin working there. Search the Scripture for wisdom in that area.

What is your "humility level" in relation to the local church? Identify one situation in which it is difficult for you to "bend low." Prepare yourself with prayer, and then purposely serve in that situation, asking God to create a servant's heart in you.

Satan hunts for Christians who are weak, only partially committed to God, afraid, unprepared, or not closely connected to the flock. Scripture shows us how to avoid becoming Satan's victim. Study the resources 1 Peter has provided. Then create a "battle plan" for future attacks. At the top of a sheet of paper, write the headings: *Area of Attack, Right Response, Right Motive.* Then, in your own words, complete your chart for each reference listed below.

1. 1 Peter 2:12   2. 1 Peter 3:9   3. 1 Peter 3:16
4. 1 Peter 3:18–20   5. 1 Peter 4:2, 4   6. 1 Peter 4:14–16

1. *The Forgotten Harvest,* Video of World Mission Night of "The 65th General Assembly of the Church of God," (Cleveland, Tenn.: World Missions Department of the Church of God, 1994). While Reverend George Chen worked and prayed in the prison cesspool in central China, the three rural churches of one hundred members which he had pastored grew to twenty-two congregations of five thousand born-again, Spirit-filled believers, all without any pastoral supervision!

2. *Spirit-Filled Life® Bible* (Nashville: Thomas Nelson Publishers, 1991), 1970, "Word Wealth: Rev. 6:15, free." Ibid., 1733, 1 Cor. 10:29, liberty."

3. Ibid., 1911, Note on 1 Pet. 2:24, 25.

4. Ibid.

5. Ibid., 1911–1912, "Kingdom Dynamics: 1 Pet. 3:1, A Word of Wisdom to Wives."

6. Ibid., 1913, Note on 1 Pet. 3:18–20.

7. Ibid., 1915, "Word Wealth, 1 Pet. 5:7, care."

8. J. Ramsey Michaels, *1 Peter,* Word Biblical Commentary (Waco: Word Books, 1988), 49:311–312.

Lesson 6/Test: Firmly Established and Abounding in the Knowledge of Jesus Christ (2 Pet. 1:1–21; Jude 20, 21)

OVERVIEW OF 2 PETER AND JUDE

Before beginning the first lesson in 2 Peter and Jude, scan the information in the charts and do a quick reading of both epistles. Then complete the purpose statement for each book and the three major themes of 2 Peter.

THE SECOND EPISTLE OF PETER[1]	
Author:	The apostle Peter (See 1:1, 16–18; 3:1)
Audience:	General readers; likely same as 1 Peter (See 1:1, 3:1)
Date:	Written A.D. 65–68
Key Words:	Know/knowledge, promise, remember, diligent
Purpose:	See 2 Peter 3:1, 2
Chapter Themes:	

JUDE
Author: Jude, probably the brother of James and Jesus (See v. 1; Mark 6:3)
Audience: General (See Jude 1)
Date: Written A.D. 65–80 sometime after 2 Peter
Key Words: The faith, contend, keep
Purpose: See Jude 3

SIMILARITIES OF 2 PETER AND JUDE
The similarities between 2 Peter and Jude become apparent in a first reading. For this reason, most scholars hold that one epistle adopted material from the other or that both used a common source as reference material. Since 2 Peter speaks of false teachers who will arise (2:1, 3:3) and Jude states such apostates have already "crept in" (v. 4), 2 Peter appears to be written prior to Jude. The use of a common source in no way compromises the hard-hitting truth each book presents.

Building a new house is an exciting time in the life of a young couple! Once they secure financing, they have many decisions to make. Will they build a one- or two-story home? How many rooms, and what size and arrangement is best? Will they use vinyl siding, stucco, or brick? Will they have carpeting, tile, or hardwood floors? Do they want wallpaper or paint? At the same time, they must determine how much of their investment they are willing to spend on each aspect of the house. How foolish it would be to spend a large amount on decorating details and scrimp on the foundation! No thinking couple would say, "I don't care what materials are used or how the foundation and frame are built."

Yet, in Christendom, we too often give little thought to the foundation and framework which establish our spiritual life and its integrity in the future. Peter warns that it is dangerous to build haphazardly. He shows that being firmly established and abounding in the knowledge of Jesus Christ, involves: (1) diligence in our personal spiritual growth (2 Pet. 1:1–11; Jude 20, 21); (2) faithfulness to the apostolic witness concerning Jesus (2 Pet. 1:12–18), and (3) adherence to Scripture (2 Pet. 1:19–21).

BE DILIGENT IN PERSONAL SPIRITUAL GROWTH (2 PET. 1:1–11, JUDE 20, 21)

Chapter 1 is of key importance to the whole of 2 Peter. Seeing his death on the near horizon, the apostle Peter exhorts his readers in the important things concerning the faith delivered to them. He describes the beginnings of faith (1:1–4), the way Christians grow (1:5–7), and the benefits of spiritual growth (1:8–11). Peter urges his readers to remember and stand fast in these things.

Read verses 1–4. How does Peter describe faith?

Even though Peter is one of the founding apostles and an eyewitness of Jesus Christ, he states that his faith and that of his readers (and us) is of the same value and kind. What do you think he means?

What is Peter's desire for these Christians and us? How is this wonderful abundance received?

WORD WEALTH

Through the knowledge of God (1:2, 3): "Knowledge" or "full knowledge", *epignōsis* (Strong's *#1922*) as used here is more than recognition or an intellectual or theoretical knowing. *Epignōsis* is a technical term related to the conversion experience which designates a specifically Christian, saving knowledge of God. This "full knowledge" is based on the truth concerning who Jesus is. It is a personal, dynamic, living, and growing knowledge which transforms the life of the "knower" to correspond to the One known.[2]

What else is given through coming to know Jesus? What is the source of this gift?

What do the "all things" Peter speaks of mean to you?

Word Wealth

Life and godliness (1:3), may also be translated "the godly life." Here, "godliness," *eusebeia* (Strong's #2150) is "piety" or "holiness" and denotes a reverent and worshipful lifestyle which is fully sensitive to God's will and obedient to His moral standards. Peter clearly states that God has given us every resource and empowerment necessary to live this kind of life.[3]

Bible Extra

Just like a healthy, newborn baby has all of its parts and everything it needs for a full life at the time of its birth, Christians are given the "godlife in miniature" at their spiritual birth. Every new Christian is given a measure of faith (Rom. 12:3), a new nature (Eph. 4:24; Col. 3:10), the "seed" of the life of God which is opposed to sin (1 John 3:9), and spiritual eyesight to see the things of the kingdom of God (John 3:3).

What added motivation does the fact that God called us "by [His own] glory and virtue" (majesty and excellence) give you personally? (1:3)

What else has been given to us by God's power? (1:4)

What two complementary works can we hope to accomplish by studying God's promises in His Word? How do these relate to the "grace and peace" and "glory and virtue" mentioned above? (1:2–4)

Write the promise recorded in 2 Timothy 3:16, 17 which parallels the thought of 2 Peter 1:4.

   BIBLE EXTRA

A baby will not grow automatically even though every life process is in place for it to do so. A new baby needs to have its new life nurtured. It must receive love. It must be kept clean. It must be fed, and fed, and fed! If this nurture does not take place properly, at best, the child will be stunted and weak, at worst, it will grow weak and die.

In the same way, Christians do not automatically grow just because they are alive. Christians, too, must nurture their perfect and wonderful new spiritual life. Not only has God provided the new life and power, like a good parent He also has given the food and the love-nurture needed for our growth! His Word cleanses, heals, and grows the spiritual life of His children. His Spirit in us and His presence in the church provide the environment of fellowship and love which fosters optimum growth (Luke 11:3, 13; John 14:16–18; Acts 2:38–42).

The Bible states that all promises given to us are "Yes" in Christ (2 Cor. 1:20), for He invites us to participate in His life and all the benefits and blessings which flow from it. What does 2 Corinthians 3:18 promise as we come to know Him more?

What two promises are prominent in 2 Peter, and how might these aid your growth? (2 Pet. 3:4, 13)

 FAITH ALIVE

Write 2 Peter 1:2–4 on a small card. Throughout the day, meditate on the meaning and promise of each phrase. When you have a break or have to wait in line, work on memorization of these verses.

Read verses 5–7. How concerned should you be about your spiritual growth? (1:5)

 WORD WEALTH

Giving all diligence (1:5): An idiom in the Greek shows that we are "to bring every effort along side of" the work God has already done and is doing. We are "to bring all diligence into" the relationship described in 1:1–4 which produces our growth.[4] This idea is similar to Paul's exhortation to "work out your own salvation with fear and trembling; for it is God who works in you both to will and to do for His good pleasure" (Phil. 2:12b, 13).

As Peter begins his discussion on spiritual growth, he says that we should add, or generously supply, seven qualities, graces, or fruit to our initial faith in Christ. Yet these elements are not added one on top of the other in sequence like layers of a cake. They are all gathered around and growing out of and with our faith. Each one supplies and enhances the other and at the same time causes our faith to grow.

Peter's idea here is not far from what James said when he stated: "Faith by itself, if it does not have works, is dead"—

useless, ungrowing, devoid of any evidence of life. And "by works faith was made perfect" (James 2:17, 22; see Lesson 2).

WORD WEALTH

Faith (1:5): After initial faith, one must grow in faith in two ways. First, "faith" (*pistis,* Strong's *#4102*) is "the contents of Christian belief concerning Jesus, the Scripture, and the Christian lifestyle." Second, it is "the divinely implanted principle of inward confidence, assurance, trust, and reliance in God and all that He says."[5]

Jude also talks about faith and growing our spiritual life. What means of growth does Jude advise? What two personal benefits does it provide? (Jude 20, 21)

BIBLE EXTRA

Praying in the Holy Spirit (Jude 20, 21): The faith-building prayer in the Holy Spirit which Jude mentions may be of three varieties: (1) spiritual prayer in one's own language (Rom. 8:15); (2) prayer with unintelligible "groanings" (Rom. 8:26); or (3) prayer in unknown tongues (1 Cor. 14:4, 14).

All Holy Spirit-infused and motivated prayers will build faith because one comes into close communion with God at such times, and the benefits of His Presence strengthen, cleanse, and make whole. God answers such prayers, so the results of these effective prayers will also cause personal edification and growth in faith. But given the context of Jude, personal prayer in the unknown tongues given as evidence of the baptism with the Holy Spirit may be indicated (Acts 2:4; 10:45, 46; 19:6). Scripture mentions several benefits of this type of prayer. (Optional topical study: self-edification: 1 Cor. 14:4; Jude 20; private worship: 1 Cor. 14:15; spiritual rejoicing: 1 Cor. 14:15; Eph. 5:18, 19; refreshing: Is. 28:12; 1 Cor. 14:21; effective intercession: Rom. 8:26; 1 Cor. 14:14; Eph. 6:18)[6]

Describe a time when praying in the Holy Spirit had the definite effect of building up your faith. (Jude 20, 21)

FAITH ALIVE

Study the eight elements below. Using a dictionary and/or concordance, write a definition for each starred (*) item. Then, after each quality, write one way in which you would like to grow.

1. **Faith** (*pistis,* Strong's *#4102*): (See "Faith" earlier in this lesson; Rom. 10:17, Jude 20, 21)
   Gained by hearing (believing and obeying) the Word of God and praying in the Holy Spirit.

   Definition:

   Way to Grow:

2. ***Virtue** (*aretē,* Strong's *#703*): This Greek word is sometimes associated with fulfilling one's purpose by fully using one's unique endowments and abilities. Some scholars think *aretē* may refer to miraculous manifestations of God's power.[7]
   Gained by listening and obeying God and His Word.

   Definition:

   Way to Grow:

3. ***Knowledge** (*gnōsis,* Strong's *#1108*):
   Gained by willing commitment to the discipline of study and prayer.

   Definition:

   Way to Grow:

4. ***Self-control** (*egkrateia,* Strong's *#1466*): This quality is involved in resisting temptation and the ability to regulate pleasure. Read Proverbs 16:32. (You may wish to review Lesson 1: "The Progress of Sin" and Lesson 3: "Submit to God . . . Humble Yourself." See Lesson 9: "Overcoming Sin Habits.")
Gained by submitting to God and His Word and resisting temptation until godly habit patterns are formed.

Definition:

Way to Grow:

5. ***Perseverence** (*hupomonē,* Strong's *#5281*): This patient endurance enables one to produce a wise and godly response to pressure and adversity. (You may wish to review Lesson 1, especially "Patience.")
Gained by prayerful trust and steadfastness to God's wisdom which allows trials to do their good work, in contrast to bitter and angry distrust which pollutes the life and negates the trials' purpose and reward.

Definition:

Way to Grow:

6. **Godliness** (*eusebeia,* Strong's *#2150*): See "Life and godliness" earlier in this lesson.
Gained by a life of regular communion with God in daily devotion, worship, and adoration.

Definition:

Way to Grow:

7. **Brotherly kindness** (*philadelphia,* Strong's *#5360*): Affection, friendliness, helpful kindness based on the family-of-God relationship. (See Rom. 12:10.)
Gained by connection and commitment to the local assembly and the corporate body of Christ.

Definition:

Way to Grow:

8. **Love** (*agapē,* Strong's *#26*): Deep, sacrificial love which is willing to suffer disadvantage and pain to work for the good benefit of another, even when there is no bond of mutuality or likeness or promise of return. (See Lesson 10.)
Gained by the work of the Spirit and the Word as one abandons self to be fully identified with the suffering and mission of Christ.

Definition:

Way to Grow:

One can have much objective knowledge without results, but applying and practicing the principles of holiness in the power of the Holy Spirit will cause growth in these graces.

Describe, in practical terms, the opposite of "barren" ("useless")[8] and "unfruitful." (1:8)

Provide the opposite inferred from Peter's list of negatives. Then, describe each practical benefit from spiritual growth. (1:9, 10)

Negative	Opposite	Applied Meaning
Spiritually shortsighted		
Spiritually blind		
Forgetful of cleansing and new birth		

Spiritual
stumbling

How does Peter summarize his exhortation on the necessity of spiritual growth? (1:10)

What corresponding abundance is promised those who diligently and abundantly supply themselves with these fruits? What do you think this could mean? (1:11)

Peter declares the wonder of the knowledge of Jesus Christ. He says that receiving this precious faith and being diligent to grow will give us more than an empty profession or a past experience. Growing Christians will have fruit, effectiveness, spiritual insight, and stability as evidence that they have built well. What a wonderful challenge and a great promise!

 FAITH ALIVE

How have "the faith" and "the promises" become more precious to you through studying this short passage?

What is the Holy Spirit calling you to do?

Whom do you know who most closely exemplifies the godly life you would like to demonstrate? How so? What can you learn from them about growing the Christlife?

Choose one or two elements from your "growth chart" of eight fruit. Decide how you will be diligent in that area(s) in the next week/month/three months. Put your plan into action. Ask someone to help you be accountable.

BE FAITHFUL TO THE APOSTOLIC WITNESS CONCERNING JESUS (2 PET. 1:12–18)

Having spoken of the great value and preciousness of the faith, and having urged his readers to new spiritual growth, Peter turns aside to call attention to the solid foundation upon which their faith has been built.

Read verses 12–15. Why the emphasis on "these things"? What is Peter's main concern for his readers? (1:12–15; see 3:1, 2)

What important truth does Peter particularly wish us not to forget? Why might that be so? (1:16; see 3:3, 4)

    WORD WEALTH

The power and coming of Jesus (1:16): "Coming" is the word *parousia* (Strong's *#3952*). This Greek word was never used to indicate Jesus' first coming. *Parousia* was consistently used by Christians to refer to the Second Coming of Jesus, when He returns in His full glory to establish His permanent residence among His glorified people. "Power" (*dunamis*, Strong's *#1411*), used in conjunction with *parousia,* denotes the powers of the age to come.[9]

What event does Peter use to prove the power and surety of Jesus' Second Coming? Why would this be a greater proof than the Resurrection? (1:16–18; Mark 9:1–10; optional: Matt. 17:1–9; Luke 9:27–36)

What authority establishes Peter's credentials as one who knows and presents the truth concerning the Second Coming of Jesus? Who is included in "we"? (1:16–18; 3:2; Mark 9:1–10)

 BEHIND THE SCENES

Apostolic authority: While the word "apostle" was used to indicate persons other than the disciples who had been with Jesus and were commissioned by Him, the apostolic authority committed to them was unique. They heard Jesus' teaching firsthand and His in-depth explanations (Mark 4:10). They were eyewitnesses of Christ who could testify of His ministry and resurrection. Thus, the teachings of the early church concerning Jesus were based upon their faithful witness and the way it enlightened Old Testament Scripture (Acts 2:42).

The writings of the apostles and their companions soon became regarded as Scripture (3:16). During the early centuries of church history, the apostles' teachings were encapsulated in brief, formal statements called creeds. Throughout church history, these creeds have been used as a test of authentic Christian faith and are today the basis of most Christian statements of faith. (Research either the Apostles' or Nicene Creed and compare it to your denominational statement of faith, or learn how the New Testament became canon.)[10]

BE FAITHFUL TO THE TRUTH OF SCRIPTURE (2 PET. 1:19–21)

The apostle Peter affirms his authority to testify as an eyewitness of the Transfiguration. Yet, he will die soon. Recollections of word-of-mouth testimony may fade or become distorted. Peter declares that there is a more sure word than even his verbal testimony as eyewitness of the power of the coming age.

Read verses 19–21. What is the sure word upon which the readers may fully rely? How long will it be the valid enlightenment for humankind? (1:19)

WORD WEALTH

Until the day . . . (1:19): The day Peter speaks of will be like the dawning of the morning. The light it brings will be so brilliant and dazzling that the light which burned in the dark will fade in comparison to it. Yet until the return of Jesus, when all darkness will be removed, this light (Scripture) will be sufficient illumination. Thus, the sure word of the prophets in Scripture should be heeded. Just as faithfully as numerous Old Testament prophecies found their fulfillment in Jesus' first coming, the whole of Scripture will most certainly be fulfilled at Christ's return. (See: Num. 24:17; 1 Cor. 13:12).

How is the absolute surety of Scripture further validated? (1:20, 21)

 WORD WEALTH

"Of any private interpretation" (1:20) has been explained in a variety of ways because of a misunderstanding of *epilusis* (Strong's *#1955,* translated "interpretation" in NKJV and NIV). The Greek form used here denotes "source" and indicates the "origin" of the prophecy of Scripture as verse 21 explains. Humans were not self-motivated, nor did they write their opinions when writing Scripture. Holy men spoke as they were "carried along" by the Holy Spirit, much as a sailboat is propelled by the wind. It is this source which gives Scripture its trustworthiness.[11]

FAITH ALIVE

Make these principles part of your understanding of Scripture:
1. Scripture is the inspired, infallible Word of God (2 Pet. 1:20, 21; 2 Tim. 3:16; 1 Cor. 2:10–13).

2. The Bible contains everything needed for salvation, faith, and the life of holiness (2 Tim. 3:16, 17).

3. Scripture is given by the Holy Spirit, taught, and interpreted by the Holy Spirit. Scripture interprets Scripture. No one verse or passage should be isolated from its context or the whole counsel of Scripture.

4. No experience holds greater authority than Scripture. Experience (vision, dream, life event, human prophecy) may come from God, Satan, flesh, the human psyche, or anchovy pizza!

Thank God for the Living Word, Jesus Christ, and the written Word, the Holy Scriptures. Commit yourself to the appropriate, and worshipful response of Bible reading and study.

1. *Nelson's Illustrated Bible Dictionary* (Nashville: Thomas Nelson Publishers, 1986), 424–425, 604–605, 823–825.
2. "Knowledge," *The New International Dictionary of New Testament Theology*, ed. Colin Brown (Grand Rapids: Zondervan, 1986), 2:392–406.
3. Richard J. Bauckham, *Jude, 2 Peter*, Word Biblical Commentary (Waco: Word Books, 1983), 50:178.
4. Fritz Rienecker and Cleon Rogers, *Linguistic Key to the Greek New Testament* (Grand Rapids: Zondervan Publishing House, 1980), 769.
5. *Spirit-Filled Life Bible*, 1492, "Word Wealth: Mark 11:22, faith."
6. Ibid., 1946, Note on Jude 20. Ibid., 2020–2021, "Holy Spirit Gifts and Power."
7. Ibid., 1919, "Word Wealth: 2 Pet. 1:5, virtue."
8. Ibid., 1919, margin note on 2 Peter 1:8.
9. Ibid., 1744, "Word Wealth: 1 Cor. 15:23, coming." Ibid., 1632, "Word Wealth: Acts 4:33, power."
10. *Nelson's Illustrated Bible Dictionary*, 78–79, 262–263.
11. Rienecker and Rogers, *Linguistic Key*, 773.

Lesson 7/Test: Alert and Unwavering in the Day of Apostasy
(2 Pet. 2:1—3:18; Jude)

As long as we live in a fallen world, counterfeiting will exist. There will always be someone who, for personal gain, will use an imitation of the real to lure others to something of no value. Banks deal with this problem every day and train their tellers to be alert to the possibility that some of the paper currency they are handed may not be authentic. Their first line of defense is to know the real. They work with and handle the real every day until the feel and appearance of the authentic is deeply engrained in their minds. When a counterfeit bill passes through their hands, an alarm goes off in their minds. Then they examine specific areas of the bill which will prove the true identity of a counterfeit.

Since the inception of the church at Pentecost, spiritual counterfeits have appeared—apostates who pass their teachings or lifestyle off as the real thing. In chapter 1, Peter urged us to abound in the knowledge of Jesus Christ, remembering the apostles' teaching and staying true to the sure word of Scripture. Now, he and Jude challenge us to be alert, unwavering in this day of deceptions. We must be: (1) alert to the presence of false teachers, (2) certain concerning the promise of Christ's return, and (3) diligent in faith and ministry.

BE ALERT: FALSE TEACHERS ARE AMONG US!
(2:1–22; JUDE 1–13, 16–19)

Jesus warned that deceivers would increase as the end of the age approached. Peter predicted and Jude declared their presence in the early church. Even more now than then, false teachers mingle themselves within true Christendom. Like Satan, the false teachers come as angels of light. Peter and Jude help us spot these apostates by unveiling their: (1) destructive heresies, (2) depraved, immoral character, and (3) dangerous deceptions.

How likely is it that you will have to deal with a false teacher? Where might these apostates be found? What do they bring with them into the church? How? (2:1, 2; Jude 4)

Despite their "Christianese," what two denials lie at the foundation of false teachers' various errors? (2:1; Jude 4)

Describe the "destructive" effect of heresies on the apostates' followers and Christianity. (2:1, 2; see Jude 4)

What can you learn from Peter and Jude's examples about how false teachers' destruction is "swift" (2:1) and active (2:3)? How apostates are "reserved under punishment" now (2:9)? What their final judgment will be like? (2:4–9; Jude 5–7)

    BIBLE EXTRA

To help you answer the questions above, look up the background references for any account unfamiliar to you.

The angels who sinned	Perhaps: Genesis 6:1–4 if "sons of God" refers to fallen angels
The ancient world	Genesis 6:1—8:19
Sodom and Gomorrah	Genesis 18:1—19:29
Generation of the Exodus	Numbers 14:26–38

What rebellious behaviors of false teachers does God especially hate and hold under punishment? (2:10a; Jude 8, 9)

WORD WEALTH

"Dreamers" (Jude 8): Jude's use of "dreamers," *enup-niazōmai* (Strong's *#1797*) may signify that false teachers are given to dreams, visions, or revelations which disclose some "new way" or "higher knowledge" than the truth of the gospel. (Jehovah's Witnesses, Mormonism, and Christian Science all began in this way.) The title also may indicate that the deceivers are lulled to sleep by their lusts and oblivious to God's judgment upon them.[1]

What illustration does Jude offer to demonstrate the apostates' disregard for authority? How do "reviling accusations" disrespect God's authority? (Jude 9; Deut. 34:5, 6; 2 Pet. 2:11; see Lesson 3: "Judgment and the Soon-Coming Judge.")

The depraved, immoral character of false teachers is further seen in 2:12–14 and Jude 10–13. List the "attitudes and motives" which can be inferred from the writers' descriptions. (2:12–14; Jude 10–13, 19)

Compare false teachers' "fruit" with the "works of the flesh" and the "fruit of the Spirit." (list Gal. 5:19–24)

Jude names three types of Old Testament false teachers. Using their accounts, describe how you would expect a "modern Cain" to pervert the gospel; a "modern Balaam" to prostitute and corrupt the gospel; and a "modern Korah" to protest the gospel?

The way of Cain:	Jude 11; Gen. 4:3–8; Heb. 11:4; 1 John 3:12
A "Modern Cain":	

The error of Balaam:	2 Pet. 2:15, 16; Jude 11; Num. 22–24; Rev. 2:14
A "Modern Balaam":	

Korah's rebellion:	Jude 11; Num. 1:1–3, 31–35
A "Modern Korah":	

According to Peter and Jude's descriptions, are Bible teachers/ministers who condone or approve of homosexual activity, same-sex marriages, and fornication false teachers? If so, are they after the order of Cain, Balaam, or Korah? How so?

Based on the writers' metaphors, how would you describe the harvest from the false teachers' ministries? (2:17; Jude 12, 13)

Read 2:18–22 and Jude 16–19 which describe the dangerous deceptions of the false teachers. If "great swelling words" are their trap, what is the double-sided bait, and who are they trying to hook? (2:18, 19; see also 2:14)

     BIBLE EXTRA

"Ones who have actually escaped from those who live in error" (2:18) are new Christians or those who are just beginning to renew their mind or change their lifestyle in some area. They have recently "escaped **error**" (*planē,* Strong's *#4106*), "a wandering, a going astray . . . in respect to morals and doctrine."[2]

What is the end-state of those "hooked" by deception? The false teachers' end? (2:19–22)

FAITH ALIVE

Over a period of time, a false teacher will reveal a pattern which shows lack of surrender to God, His commands, and His Word. Use the following guide based on Jude 8–19 to help you detect a false teacher or minister.

THE MARKS OF A FALSE TEACHER OR MINISTER (JUDE 8–9)[3]
Rebuke and reject those who: • Deny the deity and lordship of Jesus or basic doctrines.   • Habitually teach things which cannot be applied.   • Consistently leave the basic doctrines to teach "some new thing."   • Practice licentious behavior or speech.   • Show disrespect or speak ill of established authorities.   • Appear motivated by personal gain.   • Show no enduring fruit from their ministries.   • Complain and criticize others or are divisive.   • Use self-promotion or flattery for their advantage.   • Show no evidence of the Holy Spirit's life, leading, and anointing.

BE CERTAIN: THE LORD WILL RETURN!
(3:1–13; JUDE 14, 15)

Peter and Jude have shown the filthy ware of the deceivers and their undesirable end. Now Peter opens chapter 3 by exhorting readers to recall not only his witness concerning Jesus' transfiguration (2 Pet. 1:16–18), but his entire first epistle. There he showed that it is the hope of heaven which causes one to live the vigilant life of a sojourner in this world. Peter unveils the foolishness of scoffers' chidings and points his readers once more toward the certainty of heaven and home.

How does Peter describe his purpose for writing? How is a sound or "pure" mind a prerequisite to hearing what he says? (3:1–3)

 WORD WEALTH

Pure (3:1), *eilikrines* (Strong's *#1506*) describes a mind "tested by sunlight." Here, the light which has removed impurities and error-proofed the thinking is the apostles' commandment and Holy Scripture. This standard will continue to keep them free from the pollution of the deceivers and scoffers.[4]

Read 3:1–13. What major doctrine of the faith do these scoffers reject? What is their reasoning? (3:3, 4)

Based on the character, motives, and lifestyle of deceivers, why would leaving out Jesus' Second Coming be appealing? What aspect of the return do they wish to avoid? (3:3)

What other doctrines do you think false teachers like those described by Peter and Jude would want to avoid or pervert?

What three defenses does Peter offer concerning Jesus' return?

1. (3:5–7)

2. (3:8, 9)

3. (3:10)

What two things seem to be implied as catalysts for the approach of the day of God—that day when righteousness dwells? (3:11, 12)

What will the day of the Lord mean for the ungodly? The Christian? (3:7, 9–13; Jude 14, 15)

BE DILIGENT IN FAITH AND MINISTRY (3:14–18; JUDE 20–25)

The glorious doxology at the end of Jude and Peter's closing words shows that, even though we live in dangerous times which call for vigilance, our protection and success is secured by God.

Read 2 Peter 3:14–18 and Jude 20–25. In what four things must we deliberately and diligently remain? (3:14; Jude 20, 21)

As we live in the strength of God's peace and holiness, what must we be mindful to consider? (3:9, 15)

Second John 10, 11 clearly states that false teachers are not to be received or encouraged in any way. But how are we to minister to those affected by false teaching? (Jude 22, 23)

Describe how you would show compassion and guidance to unstable new converts or doubters who waiver between truth and the deceivers' errors. (Jude 22)

How is ministry to those already entrapped and defiled by false teaching different in terms of urgency and effort?

What place would the Word, warfare, and witness play in this intentional rescue? What precautions would you take with this type of ministry? (Jude 23; 2 Pet. 3:17)

What preventative does Peter offer us to combat any effect false teachers and their errors might have? (3:18)

What in Jude's closing verses gives you encouragement for this last-day battle? (Jude 24, 25)

 FAITH ALIVE

What errors in doctrine and lifestyle are particular dangers for Christians living today? How can you protect yourself and others from falling into these errors?

What motives, characteristics, or lifestyle patterns of false teachers did you also see in yourself? What measures will you take to rid yourself of these?

Learn how to witness to someone enticed or entrapped by one of the counterfeit Christian religions like Jehovah's Witnesses, Mormonism, or New Age. Use these guidelines.

GUIDELINES FOR WITNESSING

General Preparation:
(1) Witness to God's character, love, and wisdom through your everyday life.
(2) Keep yourself strong in personal devotion, worship, and Bible study.

Specific Preparation:
(1) Become familiar with the group's history and system of thought.
(2) Memorize Scripture which exposes the major errors of the cult.

Witnessing:
(1) Pray for opportunity and anointing to minister. Expect God to use His Word and your willingness. Remember His desire to save!
(2) Uncover the deep longing which made them vulnerable to the cult by asking questions and listening carefully. Find out who they are and how they got to this point.
(3) Be prayerful and sensitive to the Holy Spirit. Use God's Word skillfully as a sword, not a hammer.
(4) Share your personal testimony effectively. Cultists may be hardened to argument but open to your story.
(5) Ask if you may pray with them if a specific need has surfaced during conversation. After you leave them, pray that God will continue to move upon them with the Word and witness you have planted.

Some helpful resources:

Walter Martin, *The Kingdom of the Cults* (Minneapolis: Bethany House Publishers, 1985).

Josh McDowell, *The Best of Josh McDowell: A Ready Defense,* compiled by Bill Wilson (Nashville: Thomas Nelson, Inc., 1993).

David A. Reed, *Answering a Jehovah's Witness Subject by Subject* (Grand Rapids: Baker Book House, 1996).

Ron Rhodes and Marian Bodine, *Reasoning From the Scripture with the Mormons* (Eugene, Ore.: Harvest House Publishers, 1995).

Russell Chandler, *Understanding the New Age* (Grand Rapids: Zondervan, 1993).

1. Fritz Rienecker and Cleon Rogers, *Linguistic Key to the Greek New Testament* (Grand Rapids: Zondervan Publishing House, 1980), 805.
2. *Spirit-Filled Life Bible,* 1945, "Word Wealth: Jude 11, error."
3. Ibid., 1946–1947, "Truth-in-Action through Jude: 1."
4. Ibid., 1922, "Word Wealth: 2 Pet. 3:1, pure."

Lesson 8/Test: Enjoying Fellowship in the Truth (1 John 1:1—2:27)

In order to imagine how real the crisis of faith was for the little flock to which 1 John was written, consider this crisis that gripped a contemporary church.

Lay leaders in this Spirit-filled church became convinced that God had told them He would heal Ruth, a member in the advanced stages of cancer. These leaders initiated prayer for Ruth at each service, with the pastor and whole church participating. But instead of getting better, Ruth worsened and finally died. The church grieved and looked for ways to explain how the lay leaders could have heard from God, yet Ruth still died.

The pastor refused to blame God or anybody and challenged the church to continue in the faith that expresses itself through love (Gal. 5:6). Unfortunately the lay leaders kept insisting that the only reason Ruth had died was simple faithlessness in the church. Their simple, black-and-white view attracted others, and within two months of the funeral, about half the membership joined the lay leaders in starting a new church down the road.

Discouraged, the pastor resigned, leaving behind an unsettled little flock, troubled by nagging questions: *What if the group that left is right and we're wrong? If we didn't have enough faith for our sister to be healed, how do we know that we have enough faith to be saved? How can we know that we are living by faith? How can we know if we're doing and being what God wants us to be and do as His church?*

Although the specific reasons were different, the church to which 1 John was sent found itself reeling after a number of its people had broken fellowship and left. The members remaining were discouraged, wounded, grieving in the wake of the defection of those they had loved. The whole of 1 John is written to a broken people to encourage them in the faith and life the apostle John had delivered to them and to protect them from heresies and false loyalties.

OVERVIEW OF 1 JOHN

Read "Behind the Scenes" and study the chart below. Then complete a quick reading of 1 John. Look for repeated words, recurring themes, and statements which reveal John's purpose for writing. When you have finished, add your findings to the chart.

 BEHIND THE SCENES

The Errors of the Defectors

It seems that former members of the Christian community had fallen into errors connected with Gnosticism—a false religion which became fully developed by the second century. They were confusing believers by using John's own language and the concepts of the fourth Gospel to distort the apostle's teaching. They claimed a special enlightenment and spirituality—a higher knowledge given only to an elite few.

Because these forerunners of Gnosticism believed spirit was good and matter was evil, they found the incarnation of Christ insignificant or denied it altogether. Like later Gnostics, some may have claimed that "the Christ" descended upon Jesus after His baptism and left Him before His death, since to their thinking true God could not indwell an evil flesh-and-blood body. This error led its proponents to a self-centered life and a distorted ethic of unbridled licentiousness, false perfectionism, or an indifference to sin.[1]

1 JOHN[2]
Author: Vocabulary and style clearly indicate authorship by the writer of the fourth Gospel. Ancient testimony also ascribes the epistle to John.

Recipients:	Lack of the customary greeting and close suggests that 1 John was designed to be circulated among several house churches—probably those near Ephesus, where John spent his last years.
Date:	First John was written about A.D. 90 likely after 2 and 3 John, which do not show advanced stages of infiltration by false teachers.
Repeated words:	
Repeated themes:	
Purpose statements:	

In 1 John 1:1–2:27, the apostle John assures believers by setting guidelines for enjoying fellowship in the truth. He shows that one must: believe the eyewitness account of the incarnation and ministry of Jesus (1:1–4), walk in the light (1:5—2:11), stop loving the world (2:12–17), and reject antichrists (2:18–27).

BELIEVE THE APOSTOLIC ACCOUNT CONCERNING THE INCARNATION AND MINISTRY OF JESUS (1:1–4)

John opens his epistle by calling his readers to the foundation of Christian faith and life. He explains the weight and necessity of strict adherence to the apostolic witness concerning Jesus. His statements here become the springboard for the entire epistle, since Christian conduct, love, and assurance of salvation all find their root in sound Christian belief concerning Jesus Christ.

Read 1:1–4. (Note: The main verb for verse 1 does not occur until verse 3. If you think of verse 2 as a parenthesis, it will make understanding easier.)

Because John uses personal sensory experience to explain "the Word of life," we know that "that which was from the beginning" does not refer primarily to creation or eternity past but to what has been personally perceived and reported. Read the following verses to see how "from the beginning" has been used elsewhere in 1 John. (1:1, 7; 2:24; 3:11)

Who is John including in "we"? The apostles of whom he is the last living witness? Those who hold apostolic faith? His own churches? True Christians? Why so? (1:1–4)

What sensory experiences describe what John has known and understood concerning Jesus and the gospel? How would these prove that Jesus Christ was true flesh-and-blood? That his message concerning Jesus is not speculation or theory? (1:1, 3)

How is the relationship between the Father and Jesus described? What does this say about Jesus' deity? (1:2, 3)

What three things will be forfeited (in terms of the temporal and eternal) if one does not believe the apostolic witness concerning Jesus? (1:3, 4)

   WORD WEALTH

Fellowship (1:3, 6, 7), (*koinōnia*, Strong's *#2842*) is "close association, partnership, unity, participation with." Such unity is through the Word and by the Holy Spirit.[3]

How important is Jesus' deity and humanity? What difference would it make if Jesus were not fully human? Not fully God?

BEHIND THE SCENES

The Incarnation of Jesus and Church History: Doctrines in conflict with apostolic teaching have continued to surface in the church since John's days. This fact led leaders of the early church to meet in conference and establish creeds as measures of orthodoxy. The "Athanasian Creed" was developed in the fourth century to explain the Trinity and the Incarnation of Jesus. It and similar creeds remain standards for biblical doctrine. The Athanasian Creed reads, in part:

> "We believe and confess that our Lord Jesus Christ, the Son of God, is at once both God and Man. He is God of the substance of the Father, begotten before the worlds, and He is man of the substance of His Mother, born in the world: perfect God; perfect man, of reasoning soul and human flesh consisting; equal to the Father as touching His Godhead; less than the Father as touching His manhood. Who, although He be God and man, yet He is not two, but is one Christ; one, however, not by change of Godhead into flesh but by taking of manhood into God; one altogether, not by confusion of substance, but by unity of person . . ."[4]

WALK IN THE LIGHT (1:5–2:11)

In a glorious passage fundamental to Christian doctrine, John presents the first test of true fellowship: walking in the light. This walk involves ridding life of pretense (1:5–7), believing the truth about sin, self, and Jesus (1:8—2:2), and obeying His commands (2:3–11).

What does John mean here by "light" and "darkness"? What fundamental understanding must one have about God in order to truly walk in light? (1:5)

What pretense will keep one from both fellowship with God and others? How does John's statement corroborate Proverb's life-wisdom? (1:5, 6; Prov. 28:13)

What is the correction for this false life? (1:7)

Not only are false teachers deceived about their fellowship, they haven't believed the truth about themselves and their own sin nature. What is John's answer for those who think they have no sin principle or sinful character with which to contend? What two actions will our faithful, righteous God perform? (1:8, 9)

How does John answer false teachers' claims about sinless perfection? What is his *desire* for every Christian and the *reality* of life in this world? (1:10—2:2)

 WORD WEALTH

Our Advocate—Jesus Christ the righteous (2:1, 2): In secular Greek, "advocate" (*paraklētos,* Strong's *#3875*) denotes an attorney who represents one in court. In the New Testament, it indicates one called to the Christian's side as comforter, intercessor, legal advocate. In John's Gospel, it is used of the Holy Spirit, who is another *paraklētos* like Jesus. Here, it speaks of Jesus, who stands with us at the heavenly bar of justice and presents His own righteousness on our behalf. Jesus becomes our "propitiation" (*hilasmos,* Strong's *#2434*), the blood sacrifice of mercy which settles the account with God. (See Rom. 3:25, Is. 53:4, 5, 10, 11.)[5]

John shows the honest life of humble confession of sins to be a primary test of fellowship. What additional test does he set? (2:3, 4)

What two things does obedience prove? What two outward expressions does it take? (2:5, 6, 10)

What are the "commandments" (2:3, 4) and the one "command" which is both old and new? (2:3, 4, 7, 8)

BIBLE EXTRA

Surely "commandments" are the whole word of faith and life concerning Jesus as set forth in Scripture and apostolic teaching. The "old commandment" (2:7) which has been a part of John's teaching from the beginning has to do with living as Jesus lived (2:6) and loving fellow believers (2:10). This "new command" was made a reality in Jesus and is increasingly true of John's readers (2:8). Read about the "new command" of love in John 13:34, 35 and the new standard of selfless, serving love demonstrated in John 13:1–11 and explained in John 13:12–17.

What practical demands does this "new command" make upon you as you live and serve in your local church?

What is the best way to keep from causing a fellow believer to stumble? (2:10)

REJECT THE WORLD AND ITS ANTICHRISTS (2:12–27)

John has just taught clearly about sin and exhorted about love-motivated obedience and service. He has presented tests which prove the genuineness of fellowship with God. Now he calls attention to the true life of God demonstrated among them and warns believers to reject the counterfeits of the world and its antichrists.

What marks of genuine fellowship with God are seen in the churches to whom John writes? What is true of all? True of some? (2:12–14)

What encouragement (and warning) might be inherent in John's mention of three stages of spiritual development? (2:13)

What does loving the world prove? Why is it foolish? (2:15, 17)

What three major enticements does Satan use to lure people into his "world"? Give a practical example of each. How might knowing these facts keep heart, mind, and body clear of evil entrapments? (2:16)

Why is this trio mentioned in the context of encouraging genuine believers and combating false teaching? How are these three elements seen in the lies of the false teachers? (1:6, 8, 10; 2:4, 9, 16)

Whom is John specifically indicting, and how would you account for his use of a term of affection with this statement? To what attitude and action does the rising presence of antichrists call all Christians? (2:18)

WORD WEALTH

Antichrists and the Antichrist: "Anti" means "instead of" or "in opposition to" and describes the quality and effect of a false teacher's life and doctrine. The path of the Antichrist is prepared by a great "falling away" from the truth concerning Jesus Christ—His person and the way of salvation and life.

The final Antichrist will set up his political rule in opposition to everything truly Christian (see 2 Thess. 2:3, 4; Dan. 7:25).

What two additional tests does John present to distinguish between antichrists and genuine believers? (2:19, 22, 23)

What great reward does passing this test bear? (2:24, 25)

What discernment and understanding does even the youngest Christian possess by the Holy Spirit? (2:20, 21, 24)

In what does he **not** need the help of a teacher now? (2:26, 27; Eph. 4:11–16)

 FAITH ALIVE

Review the three errors concerning sin which John addressed:
- Sin doesn't matter; it doesn't break fellowship.
- People are basically good; I'm not prone to sin.
- I have reached or can reach sinless perfection.

How might each shipwreck a Christian's life? How would you use 1 John to answer a young convert who held one of these ideas?

Based on your study, how would you respond to the statement: "The same thing that saved you is the same thing that will keep you"?

What lures of the world are vying for your attention, energy, affection? What steps will you take to readjust your focus and passion?

How have you come to know and worship God more through the study of this passage of 1 John?

Take time to thank God for the resources He has given: the truth concerning Christ, the Holy Spirit who enables you to distinguish truth from error, the blood of Jesus which cleanses you from sin. Ask Him to help you faithfully walk in light, in love, in obedience and truth.

1. *Spirit-Filled Life Bible* (Nashville: Thomas Nelson, 1991), 1925–1926, Introduction to the First Epistle of John. Raymond E. Brown, *The Epistles of John*, The Anchor Bible (New York: Doubleday, 1982), 49–85. John R. W. Stott, *The Letters of John*, Tyndale New Testament Commentaries (Grand Rapids: William B. Eerdmans, 1988), 44–55.
2. *Spirit-Filled Life Bible*, 1925, Introduction to the First Epistle of John.
3. Ibid., 1628, "Word Wealth: Acts 2:42, fellowship."
4. "Creed," *Nelson's Illustrated Bible Dictionary* (Nashville: Thomas Nelson Publishers, 1986).
5. *Spirit-Filled Life Bible*, 1605, "Word Wealth: John 15:26, helper." Ibid., 1932, "Word Wealth: 1 John 4:10, propitiation."

Lesson 9/ Test: Confidently Abiding in Him
(1 John 2:28—4:6)

The three children scurried to stand by the door as they heard their father's car enter the driveway. They giggled and then quieted themselves as they heard his key turn in the lock. They knew that they had completed all their chores just as Dad had told them. Not once had they gotten into a fight. They hadn't scrimped on effort either! They had even done some extra things.

As Dad accompanied them from room to room, each child showed him what had been done. With confidence, they opened the closet doors and waited as Dad looked under each bed. When the inspection was completed, they held their breath as the final verdict was given: "Excellent job, kids! You've earned your reward!" The children rushed to their father, hugged him, and congratulated one another in a great tangle of joy.

How each of us would like to participate in a similar scene in heaven some day! John says that we can be confident at Christ's return if we live to please Him today. And we can be confident today in our family identity (2:28—3:3), our righteous lifestyle (3:4–10), our love for one another (3:11–23), and our discernment of truth and error (3:24—4:6).

BE CONFIDENT IN YOUR FAMILY IDENTITY (2:28—3:3)

In the last passage, John presented the idea of fellowship in the truth. Now he states that we should "continue in Him." John shows that fellowship with God should also express itself in sonship and family likeness.

What three things can we expect because of our heavenly parentage and our family likeness?
1. (2:29)

2. (3:1a)

3. (3:1b; John 15:18, 21)

How do we know that our identity is not in name only? (3:1–3)

The prospect of being changed into Christ's likeness is glorious. But how is what we perceive, know, and continue to behold in Him today important in the transformation process? What part does the hope of His return play? (2:29; 3:2, 3; see also 2 Cor. 3:18)

BE CONFIDENT BY RIGHTEOUS LIVING (3:4–10)

For any tempted to think that sin in a Christian's life is not a serious matter, John clearly spells out the nature of sin and righteousness. He shows that what we do portrays our loyalty and birth (or lack of it). John places the works of righteousness next to the works of the devil so the contrast is immediately evident.

Read 3:4–10. How is sinning defined?

What else does a pattern of sin reveal? (3:6b)

What is sin's allegiance, model, and identity? (3:8a, 10)

John does not stop with an identification of the heinous nature of sin. In order to live a holy life, a Christian must not only recognize the wickedness of sin, but understand and appropriate the tremendous work of Christ.

In 3:5, John reminds his readers of a fundamental truth which they have known all along. What does he show to be the purpose and power of Christ's first appearing?

WORD WEALTH

Take away our sins (3:5): "Take away" (*airō,* Strong's *#142*) means "to lift, remove, bear away, or carry off," and reflects the Passover lamb imagery of John 1:29. This act is more than forgiveness in which the penalty of sin is removed (see 3:6a). This once-and-for-all sacrifice has continuing effectiveness because of the present and continual purity of Jesus.[1]

In light of 1:8, 10, what is John saying in 3:6a about the effect of Christ's work upon the Christian's life? How is that confirmed by 3:7? (1:8, 10; 3:6a, 7)

How is the purpose of Jesus' first coming further described? (3:8b)

WORD WEALTH

Destroy the works of the devil (3:8): The destruction described here is not annihilation, since it is evident that sin continues to exist in the world. "To destroy" (*luō,* Strong's *#3089*) means "to loose, undo, untie, dissolve." Jesus released His children from the bondage and destruction of sin. He, in a sense, cut the knot of evil with which the devil had ensnared us so that the devil's works no longer cling to us.[2]

BIBLE EXTRA

OVERCOMING SIN HABITS

Since Jesus has cut the knot and loosed the bands of sin (3:8), the Christian does not have to remain captive to any sin-habit. Yet, like Lazarus risen to new life, one may have to unwrap the graveclothes of sin. Repeatedly yielding to wrong thinking and action creates a "sin-path" which becomes so ingrained that it is followed unconsciously. In its place, one must build a "wall of righteousness" against sin. This wall is intentionally built in the mind and actions by planned strategy:

1. **Judge the sin.** Both the motive for sinning and the character of sin must be seen for what they are. Confess rebellion to God's will. Admit the destructiveness of sin (John 10:10). Hate the sin and the fact that it hinders witness and growth in godliness. Analyze and be alert to conditions which facilitate sinning.

2. **Submit to God.** Do a topical Scripture study of the sin and the righteous way. Fully surrender to truth and the Spirit of God. Acknowledge and appreciate your resources in Him (1 John 3:5, 8b, 9).

3. **Make yourself accountable.** When dealing with ingrained sin, securing a mature Christian as coach, discipler, or counselor is wise. He/she can help one talk through offensive and defensive strategies and evaluate progress as well as form a prayer shield.

4. **Use a Word-sword.** The written Word of God was Jesus' weapon against temptation, and it is ours (Luke 4:1–13; Eph. 6:10–18). When enticed to sin, raise the shield of faith with a resounding "No!" and an affirmation from Scripture (1 John 3:8b; 4:4; 5:4a, 12a). Then pierce the heart of the matter with a Word-sword. This "sword" may be a verse addressing the specific sin or something as simple as: "You shall worship the LORD your God, and Him only you shall serve" (Luke 4:8).

5. **Build a wall.** Continue until the sin-pattern is fully eradi-
cated. Know that every successful battle is a brick laid
at the entrance to the sin-path. As the wall of righteousness is built brick by brick, the sin-path begins to fade
and the new path taken becomes habitual and auto-
matic. The resulting "wall of righteousness" becomes a
memorial and testimony of God's mighty works.

What permanent provision is given Christians to constantly resist sin and produce the righteous life? When is this
provision received? (3:9)

WORD WEALTH

Seed (3:9): Something of the very life and nature of God
is communicated to the child of God in the new birth. This
"seed" (*sperma,* Strong's *#4690*) remains and continues to
display itself. That is why it is unnatural for Christians to sin,
and a continuing pattern of sin is a strange anomaly which
contradicts the claim of a born-again experience.

BE CONFIDENT IN YOUR LOVE FOR ONE ANOTHER (3:11–23)

In this passage, John looks at the test of love again. Earlier, he spoke of love in terms of fellowship and light and darkness (2:7–11). Now, John focuses on the aspect of relationship
and life and death. As he contrasted righteousness and unrighteousness (3:4–10), he now contrasts love and hate, revealing
their ultimate expressions and source. He shows how Christians can be confident in their love for one another.

What does "from the beginning" suggest about the
importance of the love command? How does loving compare
to practicing righteousness? (3:10b, 11)

John gives three examples of "non-love" which exist in the realm of death. What is the extreme opposite of loving one another? Who is its *model*? What is its *affiliation* (source) and *motive*? (3:12)

 BIBLE EXTRA

As the first murderer, Cain becomes an archetype of all murderers. Yet he also is an archetype of the false worshiper. Read the account of Cain's feigned worship and his murder of his brother in Genesis 4:1–16.

The theme of brotherly love appears early in the Scripture. From the very beginning, it is evident that "God places a high priority on how brothers treat each other. In this passage the question of responsibility for one another emerges. Cain asks, 'Am I my brother's keeper?' The word used for 'keeper' (Hebrew *shamar*) means 'to guard, to protect, to attend, or to regard.'" God's answer to Cain's question is, "Absolutely."

"Not only are we our brother's keeper, we are held accountable for our treatment of and our ways of relating to our brothers (natural and spiritual). For Cain's sins against his brother, God curses him throughout the earth, takes away his ability to farm, and sentences him to life as a fugitive and a vagabond. This clearly indicates that unbrotherliness destines one to fruitlessness and frustration of purpose."[3]

The second level of "non-love" is hate. For whom is hating Christians an expected and typical action? Why? (3:12b, 13)

How is hate murder? How does hate differ from actual murder? Is there a moral, spiritual difference? How so? (3:15; see Matt. 5:21–28)

The third level of "non-love" is described in 3:14. In what realm does a Christian live who neglects love for fellow Christians?

John describes Christian love in terms of divine love and active love. What is the ultimate standard and archetype of Christian love? (3:16; see John 3:16; Phil. 2:4–8)

What is love's *attitude* and *personal expression* in the Christian life? Its false expression? How do you know if you qualify to be the person to meet a particular need? (3:17, 18; see also James 2:14–16)

What result can be expected from love which truly yields its compassion and resources to God and His people? (3:19, 21)

PROBING THE DEPTHS

Grieving people shaken by a traumatic event like that of John's community or persons who tend toward introspection often have an "overactive" conscience which may lead to condemnation. A sense of condemnation will squelch joy and keep one from approaching God with boldness (3:20). Thus, it is important to know the difference between unhealthy self-condemnation and the Holy Spirit's healing conviction. God is well able to discern sin. The conviction of the Holy Spirit is clear and specific (Matt. 5:23, 24). It points one to confession of particular, known sins, and leads one to cleansing and renewed, revitalized relationship with God. Condemnation or false guilt is a nebulous cloud which shrouds the heart and mind with doubt, shame, and fear. It does not point to a specific sin—a *doing* of something wrong—which can be corrected; rather it yields a sense of *being* something wrong, bad, worthless, or hopeless. God's word in Romans 8 clearly disallows such condemnation (Rom. 8:29–39).

What is the *heart motive,* the *foundation,* and the *by-product* of proactive Christian love? (3:22, 23)

How are love, truth, and obedience linked to the Spirit? (3:23, 24)

BE CONFIDENT IN YOUR RESOURCES TO DISCERN THE FALSE AND TRUE (3:24—4:6)

John shows how to assure the heart that actions toward fellow believers spring from the truth concerning Jesus and true relationship to Him. But how is one assured of one's own confession in the face of false prophets and their deceiving prophecies?

Read 4:1–6. What spirits could lie behind a prophet's pronouncements?

The Christian has rich resources to assure that he or she does not have to be deceived by a false prophet. What do we possess in terms of: (1) doctrine, (2) discernment, and (3) communion/fellowship which will help detect the presence of a false prophet? Verify a true prophet and true prophecy? (4:2–6)

 BIBLE EXTRA

Prophecy which Qualifies: "Since the heart of true prophecy is Christ Himself (Rev. 19:10), the word 'prophecy' not only defines the Bible, but confines all prophesying that claims to be true. This text shows that John distinguished the spirit of truth and error by whether the sinless glory and saviorhood of our Lord Jesus Christ was the focus.

"We should be cautious regarding groups or individuals who claim a Christian foundation: What place is Jesus Himself given? We should also reject any prophesying that preoccupies itself with mystical ideas or secondary issues. All true prophecy rests in and upon Christ, the Foundation."[4] The Holy Spirit—Who Himself witnesses concerning Jesus—is greater than Satan or error and will aid the believer in discerning and overcoming deceiving prophets (3:24; 4:4; John 16:13, 14).

FAITH ALIVE

Where do you stand in exercising your resources for discerning true and false prophets? Gullible? Asleep? Foolproof? Do you need to develop alertness to doctrinal content or the Holy Spirit's promptings? How will you do that?

How are you proving that the hope of Christ's return is alive in you? What areas in your life need to be purified? What commitments are you willing to make? How will you begin to act on that today?

Against whom in your local assembly or family do you harbor a Cain-like hatred? To whom have you "clamped off" your compassion? Confess and release that to God so that you will have freedom and success in prayer. Make it right by demonstrating proactive Christian love to that person.

Generally, how would you describe your present love relationship with fellow believers? Self-sacrificing? Compassionate and active? Indifferent? What will you do this week to reach a higher level in your Christian love?

What one truth or insight from this section of Scripture has meant the most to you? How have you come to know God more?

1. *Spirit-Filled Life Bible* (Nashville: Thomas Nelson Publishers, 1991), 1606, "Word Wealth: John 16:22, take."

2. A. E. Brooke, *A Critical and Exegetical Commentary on the Johannine Epistles,* The International Critical Commentary (Edinburgh: T & T Clark, Ltd., 1976), 89.

3. *Spirit-Filled Life Bible,* 11, "Kingdom Dynamics: Gen. 4:9, Responsibility for One Another."

4. Ibid., 1932, "Kingdom Dynamics: 1 John 4:1–6, Prophecy Not Christ-Centered Is Disqualified."

Lesson 10/Test: Manifesting God's Love
(1 John 4:7—5:4)

"How do I love thee?
Let me count the ways."[1]

These lines open a poem written by Elizabeth Barrett Browning to express the deep passion and intensity of romantic love. But we would do well to turn them toward our Lord and our fellow Christians and ask: "How do I love thee?" and then evaluate our love.

The apostle John, often labeled "the apostle of love," spends much time on the subject. Here, John deals with love for the third and final time in his epistle. It is easy to pass over the 4:7—5:4 passage on love without getting the full impact of what John is saying. Believers today can become so familiar with "God is Love" and "Love one another" that their ears are deaf to the message in the simple words. John declares that love is not only possible among Christians, but an absolute necessity. In 1 John 4:7—5:4, John presents manifesting the love of God as a test of authentic knowledge of God. The text shows that in order to truly love, we must do three things: first, know God's love revealed in His Son (4:7–11); second, let His love be matured in us (4:12–21); and third, demonstrate our love for God (5:1–4).

KNOW GOD'S LOVE REVEALED IN HIS SON (1 JOHN 4:7–11)

Read 4:7–11 from more than one translation. The passage shows the foundation upon which real love is established and the pattern and source from which true love flows.

What error does it seem John is refuting here? (4:7, 8; see also 4:20, 21)

WORD WEALTH

The God-kind of Love (4:7): *Agapē* (Strong's *#26*), a noun rarely found outside the New Testament, has a specialized meaning within Christianity. *Agapē* ("love") describes an active, self-giving love which, in goal and action, consistently seeks the highest good of another. Unlike other kinds of love, *agapē* is not based on the high value of the person to whom it is given or upon any hope of reciprocation. *Agapē* is an act of the will rather than the emotions. This love unconditionally and generously elects to set its love upon persons for their sake and benefit without demanding a return and in spite of a person's worth, attractiveness, present condition, previous actions, or consequential response.[2]

Since love is "of God" (of His Person and from Him), what two things does "doing *agapē*" prove?

1. (4:7, also see 3:9)

2. (4:7; also see 2 Cor. 3:18)

Conversely, what does *not* loving prove? Why are loving and not loving sure evidences of new birth or the lack of it? (4:7, 8)

BIBLE EXTRA

Love: The Essential Nature of God

Earlier John stated "God is light"; now he states that "God is love" (1:5; 4:8, 16). In doing so, John describes the essential nature of God. God's essence—what He is—is holiness and love. This is true of all members of the Godhead, Father, Son, and Holy Spirit. Christian doctrine describes God's essential nature of love as:

Universal and Generous: crossing all boundaries to embrace neighbor and enemy, alien and friend, the unlovely, utterly hopeless, and lost. (See Luke 19:1–10; 23:43; John 4:7–42; 8:3–11.)

Prevenient and Electing: freely and willfully bestowed, reaching out before the possibility of reciprocation exists. (See Deut. 7:7, 8; 10:15; 23:5.)

Creative and Reconciliatory: imparting value where none exists and creating the conditions needed to overcome alienation and fragmentation. (See 1 John 3:1; 4:10; Eph. 2:4, 5.)

The essential nature of God (love) cannot be known apart from His self-disclosing acts.[3]

One cannot see the *essence* of love, but one can see the *doing/action* of love. How was God's love revealed and plainly demonstrated? (4:9)

List the two ways in which God's purpose is described.

1. (4:9; see also Eph. 2:1)

2. (4:10)

WORD WEALTH

Propitiation (4:10): The atoning death of Jesus on the Cross became the "propitiation" (*hilasmos,* Strong's *#2434*), the substitutionary, mercy-sacrifice of God for our sins. As sinless Lamb, Jesus bore the wrath of God and became a covering for humanity's sin. Through Jesus' propitiation, reconciliation with God was made possible.[4]

How is God's essential nature of love and holiness displayed in His purposes? (Your answer above; 4:9, 10)

Read the definition of true *agapē* again. Why could *agapē* *not* be defined or described by our love for God? (4:10)

Is it even possible to love God with *agapē* love in its truest sense? If so, how so? If not, why not?

What action should God's self-giving love provoke? (4:11)

LET GOD'S LOVE BE MATURED IN YOU (4:12–21)

A people who know they are truly loved are secure and able to move with confidence. They do not have to constantly fear failure and rejection, but are free to grow to the fullest potential and expression. In 4:7–11, John declared that God's nature, the new birth, and a personal and growing knowledge of God should naturally lead to a manifestation of *agapē* within oneself and the church.

In case Christians might be overwhelmed by the implications of his command (4:7, 11), John shows that this love is more than an ideal. He describes how God's love grows in the life of His children.

First, John discusses the goal of God's love in us. What makes invisible God visible in His people? (4:12)

What two things does this visible expression prove?

BIBLE EXTRA

The Goal of His Love

John states that God's life and love has reached its mature expression and intended goal in us when we are loving fellow Christians. Nowhere is this goal more clearly seen than in the prayer that Jesus offered for His disciples on the eve of His Crucifixion. Read John 17 and especially note the verses listed below.

Jesus' mission and our mission	→ Manifest God's name	John 17:6a, 10b, 18
Unity and mutual love in the church	→ Manifest God's indwelling	John 17:11b, 20–23, 26

Jesus was the "brightness of His (God's) glory and the express image of His person" to the world (Heb. 1:3; 1 John 4:9). He revealed God's "name" (*onoma,* Strong's *#3686*)— God's "character, reputation, purpose, heart-intention" as it relates to humankind.[5] Now, those who are in Jesus are also drawn into God's mission and are the community in which and by which God's love and glory is revealed.

Next, John describes three witnesses of God's love which give assurance to all believers. List these below.

1. (4:13)

2. (4:14)

3. (4:15, 16)

 BIBLE EXTRA

Look up the references. Next to each write the specific work of the Holy Spirit as a divine witness of God's love.
Personal Assurance:

Romans 5:5

Romans 8:15, 16

Romans 8:23

How is the apostolic witness preserved in Scripture a special assurance of God's love for you? In the doctrine and truth it presents? In the testimony of the lives of the apostles and the early church? (4:14)

 BIBLE EXTRA

The Holy Spirit not only assures our heart that we have been drawn into God's love, He enables the apostolic witness and our own personal experience of God's love. Look up the following references. Next to each write the specific work of the Spirit in the given area.

Appropriating the apostolic witness of God's love:

John 14:16, 26; 15:26; 16:13–15

Enabling personal experience of God's life and love:

Frees from old life
1 Samuel 10:6, 9

Romans 8:2

Titus 3:5

Empowers new life
Psalm 143:10

Acts 1:8

Galatians 5:16, 22, 23

Facilitates fellowship
Acts 2:38–45

1 Cor. 12:12, 13

Eph. 5:18–21

John has shown the three elements God has given to bring full inner assurance and full growth in God's love. But what is your part in growing through the Spirit?

Through doctrine?

Through your personal experience of salvation and new life?

Describe the present and future effect of the full inner assurance of God's love wrought by the Spirit's activity, the gospel truth, and our personal salvation experience. (4:18)

John is also talking about assurance that comes from a matured outward expression of love for fellow Christians. In this sense, love has been perfected *among* us as well as *in* us (4:12, 17). What claim can be made by Christians who love this way? (4:17)

How would John 17 (See: "The Goal of His Love") and Matthew 25:34–40 relate to this confident claim?

How does the very nature and goal of a true *agapē*, which is defined by God's own self-giving, ensure the absence of anxiety in those who love this way? (4:18)

 BEHIND THE SCENES

Love Without Anxiety: During the New Testament era, several Greek words were used for love. *Eros* described the relationship between a male and female which includes sexual desire and longing. *Stergos* described the affection and sense of belonging shared by family members. *Philos* named a brotherly love or friendship—a reciprocal affection and closeness to those who are alike or connected by a common interest. Every one of these lesser loves requires or strives for a mutuality and reciprocation and is eventually destroyed by the lack of return. Only *agapē* is totally other-centered rather than self-centered. Unlike other loves, it does not nervously await response or fret over outcomes or investments.[6] (See 2 Tim. 1:7.)

How does John underline the foundation of assurance? (4:19; see also 4:10)

What is the possibility of loving God while hating a brother? (4:20, 21)

Read verses 15 and 16 again. What is the relationship between true belief concerning Jesus and love? (also see v. 10)

DEMONSTRATE YOUR LOVE FOR GOD (5:1–4)

Love is a word which is frivolously and lightly used today. One can profess "love" one minute and change his/her mind the next and "fall" out of love. But real love—the *agapē* which is from and of God—must be active, demonstrated, provable.

Read 5:1–4. In 5:1, John further connects belief and love. What is the dual effect of new birth?

How is real love for God and His children further defined? (5:2, 3; see 2:5)

Here John speaks of "commandments." In light of John's writing on obedience and love, how would you account for the use of the plural "commandments"? (2:3–11; 3:16–23; 4:7—5:4)

Why should keeping the commandments of God *not* be a heavy burden? (5:3, 4; see 3:9; 2 Pet. 1:3; John 10:10b; Ps. 1:1–3)

How would you describe the connection between faith, love, and obedience? (5:1–4)

 FAITH ALIVE

When you think about loving someone, what fears crash in on you? How would moving closer to *agapē* love help?

What is your testimony concerning the way in which God's love has "cast out fear" in your life? Caused you to love fellow believers?

Read the practical description of love recorded in 1 Corinthians 13:4–7. Ask God to point out the area(s) of expressing love in which you need to grow. Commit yourself to yield to the Spirit as God brings opportunity for practice into your life.

Take time for thanksgiving, praise, and adoration. Thank God for His love shown openly in Jesus Christ and for the victory of obedience and love your faith in Him is working.

1. Elizabeth Barrett Browning, "How Do I Love Thee? Let Me Count the Ways," from *Sonnets from the Portuguese.*

2. *Spirit-Filled Life Bible* (Nashville: Thomas Nelson Publishers, 1991), 1694, "Word Wealth: Rom. 5:5, love."

3. Charles W. Carter, ed., *A Contemporary Wesleyan Theology: Biblical, Systematic, and Practical* (Grand Rapids: Zondervan Publishing House, 1983), 120–122. *Nelson's Illustrated Bible Dictionary* (Nashville: Thomas Nelson, 1986), 656.

4. *Spirit-Filled Life Bible*, 1932, "Word Wealth: 1 John 4:10, propitiation."

5. Ibid., 1598, "Word Wealth: John 12:13, name."

6. Colin Brown, ed., *The New International Dictionary of New Testament Theology* (Grand Rapids: Zondervan Publishing House, 1986), 2:538–551.

Lesson 11/Test: Overcoming the World Through Faith In Jesus Christ
(1 John 5:5–21)

There is nothing like the thrill of victory! You can see it in the eyes of the Olympic medal winners as they stand tall and straight, faces lifted toward their country's flag and hearts swelling with the music of their nation's anthem. You can see it in the face of the recovering stroke victim as he makes his first unaided walk down the corridor of Memorial Hospital. You can see it in the glowing countenance of the soul set free who has left her burden of guilt, sin, and failure at the Cross of Christ. And you will see it in the faces of multiplied ten thousands of ten thousands of thousands as they stand before His throne crying, "Worthy is the Lamb who was slain and is alive forevermore; who has redeemed us out of every nation, and kindred, and tribe!"

John shows that true Christians are indeed victors today. We are overcoming the world through faith in Jesus Christ by: (1) believing that Jesus is the Son of God (5:5–13), (2) praying according to God's will (5:14–17), and (3) living in the victory Jesus Christ has given us (5:18–21).

BELIEVE THE WITNESSES THAT JESUS IS THE SON OF GOD (5:5–13)

In 5:1–4, John demonstrated the inseparable connection between obedience, love, and belief. He declared faith to be the key to overcoming the world. Now he defines the one who overcomes by the belief he/she holds concerning Jesus. Read 5:5–13.

Based on 2:15–17, 5:5, and the whole of 1 John, how would you describe "overcoming the world?" Who is the overcomer?

List the three ways John identifies Jesus in the opening verses of chapter 5? (5:1, 5, 6a)
   1.

   2.

   3.

How do these titles refute the false teachers' errors? Why is the authenticity of these titles absolutely necessary for our overcoming? (5:1, 5, 6a; see Lesson 8, "The Errors of the Defectors")

What claim of the false prophets is specifically noted in 5:6? How is the certainty of the fully human, fully divine nature of Jesus substantiated? (5:6)

BIBLE EXTRA

By water and blood: Since "the one who came" (*ho elthōn,* 5:6) is an aorist denoting action occurring at a particular point in the past, "by water" and "by blood" indicate specific historical events in the earthly ministry of Jesus. Some have suggested that "water and blood" refers to the substances which flowed from Jesus' side at His Crucifixion, but this meaning does not make sense with "by water only." Paired with the title "Jesus Christ," it is evident that John is using these terms to emphasize both the humanity and deity of Jesus.

If the antichrists' "by water only" referred to natural birth and human-only status, John would declare this "birth-water" also proved Jesus' divine-human nature. The preexistent "Word became flesh" by being born of Mary by the Holy Ghost (John 1:14; Luke 1:35). If the antichrists' "by water only" referred to Jesus' baptism (as is most likely), that too proved His divine-human nature. As a human, Jesus was baptized of John, fulfilling all righteousness; as deity, it was at the water of baptism that Jesus was declared God's Son with power (Matt. 3:15; Mark 1:11; John 1:30–34). In asserting the significance that Jesus Christ came by both water and blood, John marks the blood shed at Calvary as also proving the human-divine nature of Jesus. As human, Jesus bore the weight of human sin and agony and died shedding His blood. As divine, His shed blood was effective in cleansing humankind from sin and releasing humanity from death (1 John 1:7; 2:1, 2; 3:8). Thus, John proclaims that during Jesus' entire earthly life, from the first public manifestation of His ministry to His glorification at its end (John 17:1; 19:30), Jesus was *Iesous Christos*—incarnate God.[1]

In 5:6a, John deals with the objective, historical evidence which proves that Jesus is the Christ the Son of God. Now, he turns to personal and subjective evidence. What is the Spirit's function here? Why is the Spirit primary in this role? (5:6b–8, 10)

WORD WEALTH

"Bears witness," *martureō* (Strong's *#3140*) means "gives evidence, attests, testifies, affirms what is perceived or experienced," and is particularly used in the New Testament to refer to the presentation of the gospel with confirming evidence. The verb tense indicates an ongoing, present action.[2]

BIBLE EXTRA

THE HOLY SPIRIT AS WITNESS TO JESUS CHRIST	
The Spirit testifies of Jesus' Person and Ministry by . . .	
Giving prophetic foreknowledge	1 Pet. 1:10–12; 2 Pet. 1:19–21
Announcing Jesus' birth	Luke 1:35, 41–55; 2:25–38
Testifying at Jesus' baptism	Matt. 3:16; John 1:32–34
Anointing Jesus' ministry	Luke 4:18, 19
Raising Jesus from death	Romans 8:11a
Certifying Jesus' salvific work	Acts 2:32, 33
Teaching the apostles of Jesus	John 15:26, 27

Look up the following references. Jot down ways the Spirit's witness is fundamental, necessary, active, and present.

John 16:8–11 Acts 2:13–15, 37
1 Cor. 2:13, 14 1 Cor. 12:3
1 Cor. 12:4, 7 1 Cor. 12:13, 14
1 John 2:20, 27 1 John 5:6, 10
Rev. 22:17

What is the relationship between the Spirit, water, and blood? The significance of this relationship? (5:8)

BEHIND THE SCENES

Human Testimony (5:9): In ancient Jewish society, the testimony of one person was not considered valid. Two or three corroborating witnesses were required to solidly confirm a matter. John suggests that if the testimony concerning Jesus was from men, it would automatically be accepted. (See Deut. 19:15; John 3:18, 33; 8:17, 18.)

What is the ultimate authority behind the three witnesses? How serious is refusing their testimony? (5:9, 10)

What is forfeited or gained through believing or rejecting the truth concerning Jesus' Person and work? Why is this so? (5:11–12)

WORD WEALTH

Eternal life (5:11): "Life" (*zōē*, Strong's *#2222*) is used five times in verses 11 through 13. In the New Testament, *zōē* is more than physical life. It is the high quality of spiritual and moral life which comes only through faith in Jesus Christ. The Greek of verse 12 calls it "the life," noting its particular character and uniqueness. In the present, eternal life is the abundant "life of grace" marked by forgiveness of sin, the favor of God, joyful and loving fellowship in the Truth, and the benefits of salvation. In the future, it is the unending "life of glory" lived in the presence of Jesus in a new heaven and earth completely unmarred by sin.[3] (See John 10:10b, 28; 11:25, 26; 17:2, 3.)

FAITH ALIVE

Read the following verses and meditate on the life that "is in His Son" and your participation in "the life" through faith in Jesus Christ.

Victorious Life in the Son

Faith in Jesus Christ joins you:

To His victory	John 16:33; Eph. 1:20–22
To His death and resurrection life	Rom. 6:4
To His exaltation	Eph. 2:6; Col. 3:4

How does this "life in the Son" affect your outlook? To what action does it call you?

Take time to worship God, thanking Him for this life in His Son and the Spirit who enabled your faith and now bears witness in you.

PRAY ACCORDING TO GOD'S WILL (5:14–17)

In 5:5–13, John showed the necessity and great joy of being joined to Jesus Christ through faith which acknowledges His divine-human nature and appropriates His mighty work. Now he expands his explanation to include the victory which comes by praying according to God's will. Read 5:14–17.

What quality does faith in Jesus Christ impart to the believer? (5:14a)

WORD WEALTH

Confidence (5:14): *Parrhēsia* (Strong's *#3954*), in contrast to fear, timidity, or cowardice, is a confidence characterized by "outspokenness, unreserved frankness, candor, cheerful courage." It is not a human quality so much as a divine enablement manifested in spiritual power and authority to speak God's word. Such bold confidence comes as a result of being joined to God through faith in Jesus Christ and being filled with the Holy Spirit (Acts 4:31; 1 John 5:11–14).[4]

Write the two great principles stated here concerning prayer. (5:14, 15)

1.

2.

How do confidence and the principles work together? (5:14, 15)

How is what is said here like/different from what was stated in 3:19–22?

BIBLE EXTRA

Prayer which Agrees with God: "Immature faith tries to manipulate God. It looks for spiritual shortcuts and formulas guaranteed to produce an answer to any request. It regards prayer as a weapon we use to force God to make good His promises." True prayer is not based on human effort or skillful persuasion but on finding and agreeing with God's will. We request that which is His will (v. 14), then stand in faith (v. 15). Note the following lessons:

Lesson 1: *To pray with authority and success, be sure you ask according to God's will.* Subordinate your motives and desires to God (James 4:3). Search the Scripture for principles and promises which apply to your situation (2 Tim. 3:16, 17). Seek wisdom in prayer (James 1:5; Rom. 8:26, 27).

Lesson 2: *Believe God has heard your petition, and its answer is already on the way* (John 16:23, 24).

Lesson 3: *Pray with tenacity and persistence until His will is fully accomplished* (Luke 11:9–13; 18:1–8).[5]

What should be the spontaneous outflow of our confident, open communication in prayer? (5:16)

How does this underline the outcome of believing the witness concerning Jesus which was presented in 1:1–4? (1:1–4, especially 3, 4; 5:16)

What prayer is encouraged? What would likely be its content? (5:16; see James 5:14–20)

How is this act of prayer a direct contrast to Cain's action, allegiance, and motive? A fulfillment of love? (3:12, 17, 18)

How will it be answered? (5:16; see "Eternal Life" above.)

Which prayer is optional? (5:16)

Given John's ongoing discussion of the sure evidence of new birth or the lack of it, what might be the sin leading or not leading to death? (5:16, 17)

PROBING THE DEPTHS

Sin leading or not leading to death (5:16, 17): Many suggestions have been made concerning the identity of these sins, but any explanation must come from the epistle itself and the immediate context—a discussion of true faith—in which it stands. In the opening of chapter 5, John clearly showed that believing Jesus is the Christ is the foundation from which love and obedience flow, and our faith is itself the victory which overcomes the world (5:1–5). Being in the Son is equated with eternal life. Those who have truly believed are growing in Christian faith and life (2:5, 12–14). They may occasionally break a command, fail to love, or be blindsided by the entice-ments of the world, but their belief in Jesus Christ is life and is leading to life (5:10–13). Their sin does not lead to death, but to confession and cleansing (1:7—2:2). Therefore, we do well to pray for them the things that are God's will—that they might be perfected in God's life and love.

"All unrighteousness is sin" (5:17). Even though an occasional wandering from righteousness does not lead to spiritual death, it is still heinous and undesirable in the Chris-tian life (3:4–10).

On the other hand, the antichrists have willfully chosen to reject the witness of God concerning Jesus Christ (the Spirit, water, blood, 5:5–10). They have no life from the Son of God (5:11, 12), and their sin (denying Jesus is the Christ, the Son of God) and every sin connected with it (hating the brothers, disregarding the commands, habitual sinning, loving the world) are all works of the devil and darkness which are of death and lead to death. John does not command the believ-ers to abstain from praying for antichrists, but neither does he command it. Their sin is a willful rejection of the witnesses of Jesus' deity and Sonship.

LIVE IN THE VICTORY JESUS CHRIST HAS GIVEN (5:18–21)

John ends the previous section with a warning which forms a bridge to his concluding remarks (5:17). Here he recounts what believers know and have received with certainty through faith in Jesus Christ. He shows we have victory over sin, victory over the world, and victory over every deception concerning true God.

Write the first "we know" statement. Then using what you have learned in 1 John, tell what this statement means and why it is so. (5:18a)

What "new" information is added to support this state-ment of fact? (5:18b, c)

WORD WEALTH

"**Keeps**" (5:18), *tēreō,* (Strong's *#5083*), is a present, active verb meaning "to hold fast, to keep or detain (from sin), to guard from injury or loss by alertly watching over."[6]

The Greek text does not conclusively show whether it is Jesus (the One begotten Son of God) who keeps believers safe or born-again believers who keep themselves safe from the wicked one and the activity of evil. It may be that John, who often used double meanings, meant both.

Write the second "we know" statement in your own words. Use 1 John's proofs to substantiate each part of your statement. (5:19)

BIBLE EXTRA

The "world" is not the earth (see Ps. 24:1, 2), but every unredeemed thing that is part of the sphere of evil. Read these references, and describe Satan's present, temporary domain.

John 10:10; 12:31; 14:30; 16:11   2 Cor. 4:4
Eph. 2:1–3; 6:12   1 John 2:16, 17
Rev. 12:9–10 (see vv. 5, 6)

Use what you have learned in 1 John to substantiate the four "we know" statements of verse 20.

To what action should knowing true holiness, true birth, true God, and eternal life naturally lead? (5:21)

WORD WEALTH

Idols (5:21): *Eidōlon* (Strong's *#1497*) refers to "an image of worship or devotion, a false god." No empty substitute for the true God, true life of holiness, joyous Christian fellowship and love should be allowed to enter the believer's life. The wording of 5:21 emphasizes the personal responsibility of exerting effort to guard against anything false.[7]

FAITH ALIVE

How has the study of 1 John most affected your understanding of the Christian faith and life? Your understanding of God?

What insight(s) would you most like to incorporate in your life? How will you begin that this week?

1. Stephen S. Smalley, *1, 2, 3 John,* Word Biblical Commentary (Waco: Word Books, 1984), 277–279.

2. *Spirit-Filled Life Bible* (Nashville: Thomas Nelson Publishers, 1991), 1677, "Word Wealth: Acts 26:22, witnessing."

3. Ibid., 1935, "Word Wealth: 1 John 5:20, life."

4. Ibid., 1632, "Word Wealth: Acts 4:31, boldness."

5. Ibid., 1934, "Kingdom Dynamics: 1 John 5:14, 15, Prayer Is Agreeing with God's Will."

6. James Strong, "Greek Dictionary of the New Testament," *The New Strong's Exhaustive Concordance of the Bible* (Nashville: Thomas Nelson, 1984), #5083.

7. James Strong, "Greek Dictionary," *Strong's Concordance,* #1407. Fritz Rienecker and Cleon Rogers, *Linguistic Key to the Greek New Testament* (Grand Rapids: Zondervan Publishing House, 1980), 706.

Lesson 12 Test: Sharing the Cost of the Gospel Mission with Love and Joy
(2 John, 3 John)

While I was studying at a Pentecostal seminary, a group of students majoring in missions decided to test fellow students. They planted a scruffy-looking, gray-haired man near the walkway which led to the student commons area. He held a sign which read: "Will work for food." The missions students—observing from afar—discreetly recorded the reactions and responses of those passing by.

Some students bought the man a cup of coffee and/or a small snack from the vending machines. A few offered him cash. Two or three said they would help him find work or connect him with social services. But most of the students walked by the man without saying or doing anything.

The presence of the needy among us raises social, ethical, and spiritual questions which are sometimes difficult to answer. "Just in case their plight might be legitimate," one of my friends hands cash to everyone on the side of the road who carries a help sign. Another friend, having been burned by such encounters, sees all assistance as unwarranted. She fears that giving to these strangers would make her a partner to their vices. She makes it her policy to refuse all such pleas for help.

It seems that one can err on either side of the issue: being indiscriminately generous or shirking the Christian obligation of active love. In 2 and 3 John, the apostle John deals with similar issues in the church. He shows that the active love displayed in giving must find its foundation in truth. The little epistles answer the questions: What criteria should be used to determine which ministers/ministries we receive and help? And to what extent are Christians obligated to aid genuine itinerant teachers/preachers and missionaries?

AN OVERVIEW OF 2 AND 3 JOHN

Read 2 and 3 John. Write the missing information in the table below.

2 JOHN		3 JOHN
Type of Book:		
Date Written:	About A.D. 90	About A.D. 90
Author:		
Recipient(s) of Letter:		
Repeated Words or Phrases:		
Key Verse(s):	2 John 7	3 John 6b–8
Purpose for Writing:		

USE DISCERNMENT IN RECEIVING MINISTERS (2 JOHN)

Although made up of only 245 words, the second epistle of John issues a strong call for discernment within the Christian community. Not all people who claim to be Christian teachers are to be received and given the generous hospitality characteristic of the early church. The elder shows that important issues are at stake in such decisions. And the truths to be gleaned here are as relevant today as then.

 BEHIND THE SCENES

Itinerant Ministry and Hospitality in the Early Church: During the early days of Christianity, apostles, prophets, evangelists, and teachers traveled constantly to evangelize unbelievers and then strengthen the fledgling churches. The Roman roads were the Interstate freeways of today, but travel then was much harder, and there were no Hyatts or Motel 6's. Public inns were often infested with fleas and lice. Even worse, they were notorious for all kinds of immorality and vice. It became standard practice for traveling ministers to seek out the local house church and to stay in a believer's home. Soon networks of "hospitality houses" developed (Rom. 16:1, 2; Acts 16:15). Such hospitality could be costly. It not only involved providing lodging, but also daily food and the provisions necessary for traveling ministers to continue on to the next house church or mission stop (3 John 5–8).

 PROBING THE DEPTHS

The Elder and the Elect Lady (2 John 1): It seems clear from the epistles of John that "the elder" (probably the apostle John) was an overseer of a complex of house churches. The fact that he identifies himself in 2 and 3 John by title instead of personal name may be an attempt to emphasize his authority and call attention to his position as eyewitness of Jesus.

The "elect lady and her children" cannot be conclusively identified. Since both Greek words may be used as proper names, some consider the letter written to a woman and her children. However, the content of the letter seems more appropriate for a house church. In that case, the elect lady would be a hostess or leader of a house church. Then, "her children" would be her house church members, and "the children of your elect sister" (2 John 13) would be members of the local congregation to whom the elder pens this letter.

What seems to be the source of unity and affection between the elder and the elect lady and her children? (2 John 1–3)

What benefits can be expected from abiding "in truth and love"? (2 John 3)

What fact caused the elder to rejoice? What warning is inherent in this statement of joy? (2 John 4)

What is the elder's urgent command? How is it defined? (2 John 5, 6)

Based on your study of 1 John and this epistle, what truths do you think are included in "that which we have had from the beginning"? (2 John 5, 6, 9; 1 John 1:1–3; 2:7, 24; 3:11)

How important is the elder and the elect lady's shared foundation? (2 John 5, 11)

What "test" will help detect religious frauds? (2 John 7; see Lesson 8: "Antichrists" and "The Incarnation"; 1 John 2:18, 19)

How is the spiritual condition of the deceivers/antichrists described in verse 9?

List the elder's three fears concerning lack of discretion in giving hospitality? (2 John 8, 11)

1.

2.

3.

    WORD WEALTH

"Those things we worked for" (2 John 8). The verb "we worked for," *ergazomai* (Strong's # *2038*), is the opposite of inactivity and means to work, to accomplish something, to produce things.[1] In John 6:29, the author uses the same Greek verb to define the "work of God" which can be accomplished by humans: to "believe in Him whom He sent." This meaning for "those things we worked for" is also implied in verse 9. There the elder warns that one must stay true to the foundational teachings concerning Christ. If one "does not remain in the doctrine of Christ," he/she "does not have God." All that the elect lady had worked for (or believed) could be lost. The false teachers had "severed their relationship with God" by accepting an inadequate view of Christ.[2] The elder is concerned that this same thing not happen to the elect lady or her children.

What is the elder's final prohibition? What reasoning lies behind it? (2 John 10, 11)

Based on what you already know about hospitality in the early church, what activities would be involved in "receiving" and "greeting" the counterfeit teachers? (2 John 10)

 WORD WEALTH

"Share in his evil deeds" (2 John 11). The verb "share" comes from the Greek word *koinōnia* which carries the idea of close association to the extent that there is an intimate bond, a unity, joint partnership, fellowship, or brotherhood between persons or groups. The words translated "take him into/receive" and "greet/welcome" (2 John 10, 11) underline this idea of solidarity or fellowship and infer an official welcome of one who has presented himself as a teacher or missionary.

To suggest that common courtesy of acknowledging one's presence was to be denied would not be in keeping with the general teaching of the New Testament or the elder (Matt. 5:43–48). What is more likely indicated is that the elect lady was not to be associated with false teachers in name or activity by any show of partnership. Nor was she to be supportive of their ministries by giving any encouragement or material provision. Such aid was an evil work resulting in the damnation of souls. True *koinōnia* is founded in the truth (2 John 1–2; 1 John 1:1–4) and is a work of the Holy Spirit.[3]

Based on what you have learned in 2 John, how will you respond when a Jehovah's Witness knocks on your door?

DO NOT PRACTICE A "CLOSED-DOOR" POLICY (3 JOHN 9–12)

In 2 John, the difficulty concerning receiving and aiding traveling ministers was caused by undiscerning love and an indiscriminate acceptance of teachers who claimed to be Christian but did not accept foundational truth concerning the Person of Jesus Christ. In 3 John, we see the opposite scenario (disloyalty and lovelessness toward true believers) practiced by Diotrephes, a leader of a house church.

List the five actions of which Diotrephes is guilty. (3 John 9, 10)

1.

2.

3.

4.

5.

How does the elder evaluate Diotrephes' withholding of support? What conclusion does he draw based on this behavior? (3 John 11)

The elder does not mention any false teaching in connection with Diotrephes. However, he does describe a deep moral/personality flaw. Define that flaw, and brainstorm a list of characteristics one with this flaw might exhibit. (3 John 9)

What is the center or foundation of these character traits? (3 John 9)

WARMLY WELCOME AND GENEROUSLY SUPPORT VALID CHRISTIAN MINISTERS (3 JOHN 1–8, 11–14)

In our study, we have noted the dangers of nondiscretionary welcome and support of itinerant teachers, preachers, and prophets (2 John). We have also observed that "closing the church doors and pulpit" to genuine servants of God is an evil deed declaring that an individual or congregation has not seen a true revelation of the Person of Christ (3 John 11b). In the remainder of 3 John, the elder describes the minister who is to be received and the level of support he/she is to be given by believers.

 PROBING THE DEPTHS

The Greeting of 3 John (3 John 2): In recent years, the second verse of 3 John has been interpreted by some Pentecostal-charismatics as a doctrinal formula for prosperity. Some groups have created elaborate and extensive teachings from this one short verse. At times, its application has led to condemnation of those who are either sick or of meager material means, since this "formula" concludes that one's health and financial status are directly connected to the condition of one's "soul."

This extreme interpretation does not take into account the cultural and historic background of the letter or its immediate context. The cordial prayer of verse two is typical of greetings found in secular letters of the day. It promises material prosperity and physical health no more than our customary use of "Dear" to begin a letter promises romance or marriage. In today's language, 3 John 2 could go, "I pray that all goes well with you. I hope that you are as strong in body as I know you are in spirit" *(Contemporary English Version)*.

What has caused the elder's overflowing joy? (3 John 3, 4)

Fully describe the activities to which the elder specifically refers when he declares that Gaius "walks in the truth." (3 John 5–6a)

The elder is especially grateful that Gaius has extended hospitality to what group? Why might this be so? (3 John 5)

What is the elder's specific request? (3 John 6b) What factor has made this an especially urgent request? (3 John 9–11)

WORD WEALTH

"Send them forward" (3 John 6): *propempō*, is a technical term used to designate assistance given to missionaries in the early church (see Acts 15:3; 1 Cor. 11:2; 16:6, 11; 2 Cor. 1:16; Titus 3:13). In addition to supplying food, this "sending forward" in a worthy manner included washing their clothes and paying any costs necessary for them to travel as comfortably as possible.[4]

If ministers dress and live in poverty, how does this reflect on the name of the God whom they serve and to whom they look for their support? What would the opposite extreme reflect?

"In a manner worthy of God" (3 John 6b) might mean "as a service rendered to God Himself," or "with a loving generosity that brings glory to God." Taking both ideas into account, describe the actions you see as appropriate in sending an evangelist or teacher to his/her next ministry post today.

What is the motivation behind the itinerant ministers' service? (3 John 7)

What additional reason for supporting these itinerant ministers is given? (3 John 7)

Read Jesus' instructions in Matthew 10:7–14. What double blessing might be set in motion by the "illogical action" of going out empty-handed?

What is the third reason that ministers should be treated with the warmest hospitality? (3 John 8)

 BIBLE EXTRA

Third John 8 gives a strong command for ministry support. There "ought" bears the idea of a moral necessity and a divine obligation. Read the following references. Then list additional reasons you and your church should welcome faithful visiting ministers and give them material support.

3 John 8

Matthew 10:40–42

Matthew 25:37–40

Mark 9:41

What two partnerships does one enter who supports valid Christian enterprises? (3 John 8b, 11b)

What three witnesses declare Demetrius a proper candidate for Gaius's generous hospitality? (3 John 12)

How would you translate the three facts concerning Demetrius into a modern "test" of eligibility for acceptance and facilitation of one's ministry? (3 John 12)

 FAITH ALIVE

As a review, list the three major teachings of 2 and 3 John. (See section headings.)

1.

2.

3.

Would you say you and your local church are more like the elect lady, Gaius, or Diotrephes in receiving and supporting traveling ministers? Why?

Describe your/your church's support of missions. How does this picture line up with the message of 2 and 3 John?

If itinerant ministers who meet the test are to be treated with such lavish hospitality, how would you apply this same principle to facilitating and mentoring those newly called or being trained for ministry?

Take time to thank God for gifting the body of Christ with apostles, prophets, evangelists, pastors, and teachers who truly serve for the sake of the Name. Thank Him for the joint harvest you may reap through partnership with them in the gospel.

1. *Spirit-Filled Life Bible* (Nashville: Thomas Nelson Publishers, 1991), 1578, "Word Wealth: John 3:21, been done."
2. Ibid., 1938, Note on 2 John 9.
3. Ibid., 1628, "Word Wealth: Acts 2:42, fellowship." John R. W. Stott, *The Letters of John*, Tyndale New Testament Commentaries (Grand Rapids: Eerdmans Publishing Company, 1990), 214–217.
4. I. Howard Marshall, *The Epistles of John*, The New International Commentary on the New Testament (Grand Rapids: William B. Eerdmans Publishing Company, 1978), 85–86.

SPIRIT-FILLED LIFE® BIBLE DISCOVERY GUIDE SERIES

B 1   Genesis 0-8407-8515-1
B 2   Exodus, Leviticus, Numbers, Deuteronomy
        0-8407-8513-5
B 3   Joshua & Judges 0-7852-1242-6
B 4   Ruth & Esther 0-7852-1133-0
B 5   1 & 2 Samuel, 1 Chronicles 0-7852-1243-4
B 6   1 & 2 Kings, 2 Chronicles 0-7852-1257-4
B 7   Ezra & Nehemiah 0-7852-1258-2
B 8* Job, Ecclesiastes, Song of Songs
B 9   Psalms 0-8407-8347-7
B10   Proverbs 0-7852-1167-5
B11   Isaiah 0-7852-1168-3
B12* Jeremiah, Lamentations, Ezekiel
B13   Daniel & Revelation 0-8407-2081-5
B14   Hosea, Joel, Amos, Obadiah, Jonah, Micah, Nahum,
        Habakkuk, Zephaniah, Haggai, Zechariah, Malachi
        0-8407-2093-9
B15   Matthew, Mark, Luke 0-8407-2090-4
B16   John 0-8407-8349-3
B17   Acts 0-8407-8345-0
B18   Romans 0-8407-8350-7
B19   1 Corinthians 0-8407-8514-3
B20   2 Corinthians, 1 & 2 Timothy, Titus 0-7852-1204-3
B21   Galatians, 1 & 2 Thessalonians 0-7852-1134-9
B22   Ephesians, Philippians, Colossians, Philemon
        0-8407-8512-7
B23   Hebrews 0-8407-2082-3
B24   James, 1 & 2 Peter, 1–3 John, Jude 0-7852-1205-1
B25* Getting to the Heart of the Bible (Key Themes: Basics
        of Bible Study)

*Coming Soon

SPIRIT-FILLED LIFE® KINGDOM DYNAMICS STUDY GUIDES

K 1   People of the Spirit: Gifts, Fruit, and Fullness of the Holy Spirit 0-8407-8431-7

K 2   Kingdom Warfare: Prayer, Spiritual Warfare, and the Ministry of Angels 0-8407-8433-3

K 3   God's Way to Wholeness: Divine Healing by the Power of the Holy Spirit 0-8407-8430-9

K 4   Life in the Kingdom: Foundations of the Faith 0-8407-8432-5

K 5   Focusing on the Future: Key Prophecies and Practical Living 0-8407-8517-8

K 6   Toward More Glorious Praise: Power Principles for Faith-Filled People 0-8407-8518-6

K 7   Bible Ministries for Women: God's Daughters and God's Work 0-8407-8519-4

K 8   People of the Covenant: God's New Covenant for Today 0-8407-8520-8

K 9   Answering the Call to Evangelism: Spreading the Good News to Everyone 0-8407-2096-3

K10   Spirit-Filled Family: Holy Wisdom to Build Happy Homes 0-8407-2085-8

K11   Appointed to Leadership: God's Principles for Spiritual Leaders 0-8407-2083-1

K12   Power Faith: Balancing Faith in Words and Work 0-8407-2094-7

K13   Race & Reconciliation: Healing the Wounds, Winning the Harvest 0-7852-1131-4

K14   Praying in the Spirit: Heavenly Resources for Praise and Intercession 0-7852-1141-1

OTHER SPIRIT-FILLED LIFE® STUDY RESOURCES

Spirit-Filled Life® Bible, available in several bindings and in NKJV and KJV.
Spirit-Filled Life® Bible for Students
Hayford's Bible Handbook 0-8407-8359-0